READE THE TEXTS AGAIN. ⑤

Put the facts together. What questions were answered about the moon?

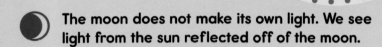

MA_ _CENT

- ☾ The moon does not make its own light. We see light from the sun reflected off of the moon.

- ☾ The moon has lots of craters. Meteoroids that crash into the moon form them.

- ☾ The moon has no wind or weather. The footsteps left by astronauts will stay on the moon for millions of years.

- ☾ The moon has extreme temperatures. The temperature can reach 253°F (123°C) on the side where the sun shines. It can get as cold as -387°F (-233°C) on the dark side of the moon.

- ☾ Sometimes the moon moves between Earth and the sun and blocks the sunlight. This is a solar eclipse.

WRITE ABOUT IT.

Do you ever look up at the moon at night? What do _____ out? ⑥

EARTH'S SOLE Satellite

Have you ever wondered about the brightly shining satellite in the night sky? The moon has kept us wondering for years.

Many scientists believe the moon and Earth formed at the same time. That was 4.5 billion years ago! A small planet the size of Mars hit Earth. Some big pieces were knocked loose. They formed a cloud. Over time, the pieces melted together. Then, they cooled down. This became the moon.

For years, we could only look at the moon. Now, we can walk on it! In 1609, a man named Galileo made a telescope. He could study the surface of the moon. But, it wasn't until 1969 that an American astronaut walked on the moon. Neil Armstrong said these famous words, "That's one small step for a man, one giant leap for mankind."

The moon is airless, waterless, and lifeless. Yet, it affects our lives in many ways.

Read the titles. Scan the texts. Look at the pictures and chart. ①

What do you think you will learn about the **MOON?**

Waxing? Waning? WHAT?

Refer to the illustrations and photos to help you answer questions about the texts.

How did the moon help to inspire the calendar?

④

VOCABULARY

eclipse:
when one object in space blocks another one from view

meteoroid:
a small mass of stone or metal in outer space

satellite:
an object in space that orbits around another larger object

wane:
to become smaller in size

wax:
to become larger in size

②

Why does the moon change its looks? It goes through phases. The moon's orbit around Earth causes the phases. The new moon is first. It cannot be seen from Earth. Next, the waxing moon appears as a crescent. Then, a full moon appears. Finally, the waning moon appears. The moon goes through four phases about every 29 days, or one lunar month.

American Indians living a few hundred years ago gave each full moon a nickname. This is how they kept track of seasons. For example, the Wolf Moon appeared in January when wolves howled in hunger. The Strawberry Moon appeared in June. That was the time to pick strawberries. The Hunter's Moon appeared in October. That was when the leaves fell and it was time to hunt and store food for winter.

In what month were you born? Think about how the full moon nickname fits that month.

Read the texts. What questions do you have? Write them
- in the margins,
- in a notebook,
- or on self-stick notes.

Discuss the questions with others.

③

In AMERICAN FOLKLORE, the FULL MOON for each month has been given a NICKNAME.

JANUARY
Wolf Moon

FEBRUARY
Snow Moon

MARCH
Worm Moon

APRIL
Pink Moon

MAY
Flower Moon

JUNE
Strawberry Moon

JULY
Buck Moon

AUGUST
Sturgeon Moon

SEPTEMBER
Corn Moon

OCTOBER
Hunter's Moon

NOVEMBER
Beaver Moon

DECEMBER
Cold Moon

Catching a Tidal Wave?

Thank the MOON!

Did you know that if there were no moon, we would have no tides? The moon's gravity pulls on Earth. This pull makes the oceans rise up toward the moon as it passes over them. As Earth rotates, the oceans move up and down depending on where the moon is. This movement is what causes tides. During high tides, Earth also bulges out an inch or two because the oceans rise! But, it's not enough for us to notice.

MAGNIFICENT Moon

- The moon does not make its own light. We see light from the sun reflected off of the moon.

- The moon has lots of craters. Meteoroids that crash into the moon form them.

- The moon has no wind or weather. The footsteps left by astronauts will stay on the moon for millions of years.

- The moon has extreme temperatures. The temperature can reach 253°F (123°C) on the side where the sun shines. It can get as cold as -387°F (-233°C) on the dark side of the moon.

- Sometimes the moon moves between Earth and the sun and blocks the sunlight. This is a solar eclipse.

WRITE ABOUT IT.
Do you ever look up at the moon at night? What do you think about? ⑥

© Carson-Dellosa CD-104930

QUESTION to wonder about information in the text

EARTH'S SOLE Satellite

Have you ever wondered about the brightly shining satellite in the night sky? The moon has kept us wondering for years.

Many scientists believe the moon and Earth formed at the same time. That was 4.5 billion years ago! A small planet the size of Mars hit Earth. Some big pieces were knocked loose. They formed a cloud. Over time, the pieces melted together. Then, they cooled down. This became the moon.

For years, we could only look at the moon. Now, we can walk on it! In 1609, a man named Galileo made a telescope. He could study the surface of the moon. But, it wasn't until 1969 that an American astronaut walked on the moon. Neil Armstrong said these famous words, "That's one small step for a man, one giant leap for mankind."

The moon is airless, waterless, and lifeless. Yet, it affects our lives in many ways.

Read the titles. Scan the texts. Look at the pictures and chart. ①

What do you think you will learn about the MOON?

Waxing? Waning? WHAT?

Refer to the illustrations and photos to help you answer questions about the texts. ④

How did the moon help to inspire the calendar?

VOCABULARY

eclipse:
when one object in space blocks another one from view

meteoroid:
a small mass of stone or metal in outer space

satellite:
an object in space that orbits around another larger object

wane:
to become smaller in size

wax:
to become larger in size

②

Read the texts. What questions do you have? Write them

- in the margins,
- in a notebook,
- or on self-stick notes.

Discuss the questions with others.

③

Why does the moon change its looks? It goes through phases. The moon's orbit around Earth causes the phases. The new moon is first. It cannot be seen from Earth. Next, the waxing moon appears as a crescent. Then, a full moon appears. Finally, the waning moon appears. The moon goes through four phases about every 29 days, or one lunar month.

American Indians living a few hundred years ago gave each full moon a nickname. This is how they kept track of seasons. For example, the Wolf Moon appeared in January when wolves howled in hunger. The Strawberry Moon appeared in June. That was the time to pick strawberries. The Hunter's Moon appeared in October. That was when the leaves fell and it was time to hunt and store food for winter.

In what month were you born? Think about how the full moon nickname fits that month.

In AMERICAN FOLKLORE, the FULL MOON for each month has been given a NICKNAME.

JANUARY
Wolf Moon

FEBRUARY
Snow Moon

MARCH
Worm Moon

APRIL
Pink Moon

MAY
Flower Moon

JUNE
Strawberry Moon

JULY
Buck Moon

AUGUST
Sturgeon Moon

SEPTEMBER
Corn Moon

OCTOBER
Hunter's Moon

NOVEMBER
Beaver Moon

DECEMBER
Cold Moon

Catching a Tidal Wave?
Thank the MOON!

Did you know that if there were no moon, we would have no tides? The moon's gravity pulls on Earth. This pull makes the oceans rise up toward the moon as it passes over them. As Earth rotates, the oceans move up and down depending on where the moon is. This movement is what causes tides. During high tides, Earth also bulges out an inch or two because the oceans rise! But, it's not enough for us to notice.

MAGNIFICENT
Moon

- The moon does not make its own light. We see light from the sun reflected off of the moon.

- The moon has lots of craters. Meteoroids that crash into the moon form them.

- The moon has no wind or weather. The footsteps left by astronauts will stay on the moon for millions of years.

- The moon has extreme temperatures. The temperature can reach 253°F (123°C) on the side where the sun shines. It can get as cold as -387°F (-233°C) on the dark side of the moon.

- Sometimes the moon moves between Earth and the sun and blocks the sunlight. This is a solar eclipse.

WRITE ABOUT IT.
Do you ever look up at the moon at night? What do you think about? 6

QUESTION to wonder about information in the text

EARTH'S SOLE Satellite

Have you ever wondered about the brightly shining satellite in the night sky? The moon has kept us wondering for years.

Many scientists believe the moon and Earth formed at the same time. That was 4.5 billion years ago! A small planet the size of Mars hit Earth. Some big pieces were knocked loose. They formed a cloud. Over time, the pieces melted together. Then, they cooled down. This became the moon.

For years, we could only look at the moon. Now, we can walk on it! In 1609, a man named Galileo made a telescope. He could study the surface of the moon. But, it wasn't until 1969 that an American astronaut walked on the moon. Neil Armstrong said these famous words, "That's one small step for a man, one giant leap for mankind."

The moon is airless, waterless, and lifeless. Yet, it affects our lives in many ways.

Read the titles. Scan the texts. Look at the pictures and chart. 1

What do you think you will learn about the **MOON?**

Waxing? Waning? WHAT?

Why does the moon change its looks? It goes through phases. The moon's orbit around Earth causes the phases. The new moon is first. It cannot be seen from Earth. Next, the waxing moon appears as a crescent. Then, a full moon appears. Finally, the waning moon appears. The moon goes through four phases about every 29 days, or one lunar month.

American Indians living a few hundred years ago gave each full moon a nickname. This is how they kept track of seasons. For example, the Wolf Moon appeared in January when wolves howled in hunger. The Strawberry Moon appeared in June. That was the time to pick strawberries. The Hunter's Moon appeared in October. That was when the leaves fell and it was time to hunt and store food for winter.

In what month were you born? Think about how the full moon nickname fits that month.

VOCABULARY

eclipse:
   when one object in space blocks another one from view

meteoroid:
   a small mass of stone or metal in outer space

satellite:
   an object in space that orbits around another larger object

wane:
   to become smaller in size

wax:
   to become larger in size

(2)

Read the texts. What questions do you have? Write them
- in the margins,
- in a notebook,
- or on self-stick notes.

Discuss the questions with others.

(3)

In **AMERICAN FOLKLORE**, the **FULL MOON** for each month has been given a **NICKNAME**.

JANUARY
Wolf Moon

FEBRUARY
Snow Moon

MARCH
Worm Moon

APRIL
Pink Moon

MAY
Flower Moon

JUNE
Strawberry Moon

JULY
Buck Moon

AUGUST
Sturgeon Moon

SEPTEMBER
Corn Moon

OCTOBER
Hunter's Moon

NOVEMBER
Beaver Moon

DECEMBER
Cold Moon

Refer to the illustrations and photos to help you answer questions about the texts.

(4)

How did the moon help to inspire the calendar?

Catching a Tidal Wave?
Thank the MOON!

Did you know that if there were no moon, we would have no tides? The moon's gravity pulls on Earth. This pull makes the oceans rise up toward the moon as it passes over them. As Earth rotates, the oceans move up and down depending on where the moon is. This movement is what causes tides. During high tides, Earth also bulges out an inch or two because the oceans rise! But, it's not enough for us to notice.

MAGNIFICENT
Moon

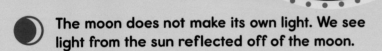

- The moon does not make its own light. We see light from the sun reflected off of the moon.

- The moon has lots of craters. Meteoroids that crash into the moon form them.

- The moon has no wind or weather. The footsteps left by astronauts will stay on the moon for millions of years.

- The moon has extreme temperatures. The temperature can reach 253°F (123°C) on the side where the sun shines. It can get as cold as -387°F (-233°C) on the dark side of the moon.

- Sometimes the moon moves between Earth and the sun and blocks the sunlight. This is a solar eclipse.

WRITE ABOUT IT.
Do you ever look up at the moon at night? What do you think about? 6

QUESTION to wonder
about information in the text

EARTH'S SOLE
Satellite

Have you ever wondered about the brightly shining satellite in the night sky? The moon has kept us wondering for years.

Many scientists believe the moon and Earth formed at the same time. That was 4.5 billion years ago! A small planet the size of Mars hit Earth. Some big pieces were knocked loose. They formed a cloud. Over time, the pieces melted together. Then, they cooled down. This became the moon.

For years, we could only look at the moon. Now, we can walk on it! In 1609, a man named Galileo made a telescope. He could study the surface of the moon. But, it wasn't until 1969 that an American astronaut walked on the moon. Neil Armstrong said these famous words, "That's one small step for a man, one giant leap for mankind."

The moon is airless, waterless, and lifeless. Yet, it affects our lives in many ways.

Read the titles. Scan the texts. Look at the pictures and chart. 1

What do you think you will learn about the MOON?

Waxing? Waning? WHAT?

VOCABULARY

eclipse:
  when one object in space blocks another one from view

meteoroid:
  a small mass of stone or metal in outer space

satellite:
  an object in space that orbits around another larger object

wane:
  to become smaller in size

wax:
  to become larger in size

②

Why does the moon change its looks? It goes through phases. The moon's orbit around Earth causes the phases. The new moon is first. It cannot be seen from Earth. Next, the waxing moon appears as a crescent. Then, a full moon appears. Finally, the waning moon appears. The moon goes through four phases about every 29 days, or one lunar month.

American Indians living a few hundred years ago gave each full moon a nickname. This is how they kept track of seasons. For example, the Wolf Moon appeared in January when wolves howled in hunger. The Strawberry Moon appeared in June. That was the time to pick strawberries. The Hunter's Moon appeared in October. That was when the leaves fell and it was time to hunt and store food for winter.

In what month were you born? Think about how the full moon nickname fits that month.

Refer to the illustrations and photos to help you answer questions about the texts.

How did the moon help to inspire the calendar?

④

Read the texts. What questions do you have? Write them

- in the margins,
- in a notebook,
- or on self-stick notes.

Discuss the questions with others.

③

Catching a Tidal Wave? Thank the MOON!

Did you know that if there were no moon, we would have no tides? The moon's gravity pulls on Earth. This pull makes the oceans rise up toward the moon as it passes over them. As Earth rotates, the oceans move up and down depending on where the moon is. This movement is what causes tides. During high tides, Earth also bulges out an inch or two because the oceans rise! But, it's not enough for us to notice.

In AMERICAN FOLKLORE, the FULL MOON for each month has been given a NICKNAME.

 JANUARY Wolf Moon

 FEBRUARY Snow Moon

 MARCH Worm Moon

 APRIL Pink Moon

 MAY Flower Moon

 JUNE Strawberry Moon

 JULY Buck Moon

 AUGUST Sturgeon Moon

 SEPTEMBER Corn Moon

 OCTOBER Hunter's Moon

 NOVEMBER Beaver Moon

   DECEMBER Cold Moon

MAGNIFICENT
Moon

- The moon does not make its own light. We see light from the sun reflected off of the moon.

- The moon has lots of craters. Meteoroids that crash into the moon form them.

- The moon has no wind or weather. The footsteps left by astronauts will stay on the moon for millions of years.

- The moon has extreme temperatures. The temperature can reach 253°F (123°C) on the side where the sun shines. It can get as cold as -387°F (-233°C) on the dark side of the moon.

- Sometimes the moon moves between Earth and the sun and blocks the sunlight. This is a solar eclipse.

WRITE ABOUT IT.
Do you ever look up at the moon at night? What do you think about? ⑥

QUESTION to wonder about information in the text

EARTH'S SOLE Satellite

Have you ever wondered about the brightly shining satellite in the night sky? The moon has kept us wondering for years.

Many scientists believe the moon and Earth formed at the same time. That was 4.5 billion years ago! A small planet the size of Mars hit Earth. Some big pieces were knocked loose. They formed a cloud. Over time, the pieces melted together. Then, they cooled down. This became the moon.

For years, we could only look at the moon. Now, we can walk on it! In 1609, a man named Galileo made a telescope. He could study the surface of the moon. But, it wasn't until 1969 that an American astronaut walked on the moon. Neil Armstrong said these famous words, "That's one small step for a man, one giant leap for mankind."

The moon is airless, waterless, and lifeless. Yet, it affects our lives in many ways.

Read the titles. Scan the texts. Look at the pictures and chart. ①

What do you think you will learn about the **MOON?**

Waxing? Waning? WHAT?

Why does the moon change its looks? It goes through phases. The moon's orbit around Earth causes the phases. The new moon is first. It cannot be seen from Earth. Next, the waxing moon appears as a crescent. Then, a full moon appears. Finally, the waning moon appears. The moon goes through four phases about every 29 days, or one lunar month.

American Indians living a few hundred years ago gave each full moon a nickname. This is how they kept track of seasons. For example, the Wolf Moon appeared in January when wolves howled in hunger. The Strawberry Moon appeared in June. That was the time to pick strawberries. The Hunter's Moon appeared in October. That was when the leaves fell and it was time to hunt and store food for winter.

In what month were you born? Think about how the full moon nickname fits that month.

Refer to the illustrations and photos to help you answer questions about the texts.

④

How did the moon help to inspire the calendar?

VOCABULARY

eclipse:
when one object in space blocks another one from view

meteoroid:
a small mass of stone or metal in outer space

satellite:
an object in space that orbits around another larger object

wane:
to become smaller in size

②

wax:
to become larger in size

Read the texts. What questions do you have? Write them
- in the margins,
- in a notebook,
- or on self-stick notes.

Discuss the questions with others.

③

In AMERICAN FOLKLORE, the FULL MOON for each month has been given a NICKNAME.

 JANUARY Wolf Moon

 FEBRUARY Snow Moon

 MARCH Worm Moon

 APRIL Pink Moon

 MAY Flower Moon

 JUNE Strawberry Moon

 JULY Buck Moon

 AUGUST Sturgeon Moon

 SEPTEMBER Corn Moon

 OCTOBER Hunter's Moon

 NOVEMBER Beaver Moon

 DECEMBER Cold Moon

Catching a Tidal Wave?
Thank the MOON!

Did you know that if there were no moon, we would have no tides? The moon's gravity pulls on Earth. This pull makes the oceans rise up toward the moon as it passes over them. As Earth rotates, the oceans move up and down depending on where the moon is. This movement is what causes tides. During high tides, Earth also bulges out an inch or two because the oceans rise! But, it's not enough for us to notice.

READE THE TEXTS AGAIN. ⑤
Put the facts together. What questions were
answered about the moon?

MAGNIFICENT
Moon

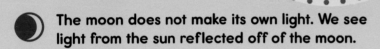

- The moon does not make its own light. We see light from the sun reflected off of the moon.

- The moon has lots of craters. Meteoroids that crash into the moon form them.

- The moon has no wind or weather. The footsteps left by astronauts will stay on the moon for millions of years.

- The moon has extreme temperatures. The temperature can reach 253°F (123°C) on the side where the sun shines. It can get as cold as -387°F (-233°C) on the dark side of the moon.

- Sometimes the moon moves between Earth and the sun and blocks the sunlight. This is a solar eclipse.

WRITE ABOUT IT.
Do you ever look up at the moon at night? What do
you think about? ⑥

EARTH'S SOLE Satellite

Have you ever wondered about the brightly shining satellite in the night sky? The moon has kept us wondering for years.

Many scientists believe the moon and Earth formed at the same time. That was 4.5 billion years ago! A small planet the size of Mars hit Earth. Some big pieces were knocked loose. They formed a cloud. Over time, the pieces melted together. Then, they cooled down. This became the moon.

For years, we could only look at the moon. Now, we can walk on it! In 1609, a man named Galileo made a telescope. He could study the surface of the moon. But, it wasn't until 1969 that an American astronaut walked on the moon. Neil Armstrong said these famous words, "That's one small step for a man, one giant leap for mankind."

The moon is airless, waterless, and lifeless. Yet, it affects our lives in many ways.

Read the titles. Scan
the texts. Look at the
pictures and chart. ①

What do you think
you will learn about
the **MOON?**

Waxing? Waning? WHAT?

Refer to the illustrations and photos to help you answer questions about the texts.

④

How did the moon help to inspire the calendar?

VOCABULARY

eclipse:
when one object in space blocks another one from view

meteoroid:
a small mass of stone or metal in outer space

satellite:
an object in space that orbits around another larger object

wane:
to become smaller in size

wax:
to become larger in size

②

Why does the moon change its looks? It goes through phases. The moon's orbit around Earth causes the phases. The new moon is first. It cannot be seen from Earth. Next, the waxing moon appears as a crescent. Then, a full moon appears. Finally, the waning moon appears. The moon goes through four phases about every 29 days, or one lunar month.

American Indians living a few hundred years ago gave each full moon a nickname. This is how they kept track of seasons. For example, the Wolf Moon appeared in January when wolves howled in hunger. The Strawberry Moon appeared in June. That was the time to pick strawberries. The Hunter's Moon appeared in October. That was when the leaves fell and it was time to hunt and store food for winter.

In what month were you born? Think about how the full moon nickname fits that month.

Catching a Tidal Wave? Thank the MOON!

Did you know that if there were no moon, we would have no tides? The moon's gravity pulls on Earth. This pull makes the oceans rise up toward the moon as it passes over them. As Earth rotates, the oceans move up and down depending on where the moon is. This movement is what causes tides. During high tides, Earth also bulges out an inch or two because the oceans rise! But, it's not enough for us to notice.

Read the texts. What questions do you have? Write them
- in the margins,
- in a notebook,
- or on self-stick notes.

Discuss the questions with others.

③

In AMERICAN FOLKLORE, the FULL MOON for each month has been given a NICKNAME.

JANUARY Wolf Moon

FEBRUARY Snow Moon

MARCH Worm Moon

APRIL Pink Moon

MAY Flower Moon

JUNE Strawberry Moon

JULY Buck Moon

AUGUST Sturgeon Moon

SEPTEMBER Corn Moon

OCTOBER Hunter's Moon

NOVEMBER Beaver Moon

DECEMBER Cold Moon

READ THE TEXTS AGAIN. ⑤

Put the facts together. How did mail delivery develop through the years?

MAIL

Takes Flight

PAR AVION

AIRMAIL

Airplanes were used during World War I. Planes were very helpful to our military. They could deliver supplies to faraway places. So, it made sense that airplanes should be used to carry mail too.

The US Congress put aside some money in 1918. It was used to set up airmail routes. The first route was between New York City, New York and Washington, D.C. The route had one stop at Philadelphia, Pennsylvania. The first airmail trip took just over three hours. The delivery included a letter for the president.

"In rain or shine, snow or sleet, mail is delivered." This is a motto for mail carriers. But, the rain, snow, and sleet were problems for early airmail. Over time, these bumps in the sky were worked out. Airmail soon became a popular form of mail delivery.

WRITE ABOUT IT. ⑥

Imagine you received a letter from Brazil. What mail delivery system do you think was used? What makes you think so?

QUESTION to wonder about information in the text

IT'S IN THE MAIL

How do you send mail? Do you click "send" to fire off an email? Or do you like to use snail mail?

Email lets people send notes around the world or around the corner very quickly. Some teachers use email to communicate with parents. Sorry, kids—no more notes getting lost in backpacks!

But, mail wasn't always as simple as sending an email. Have you ever received a card or letter in your mailbox? How did it get there? It may have traveled by truck. It may have traveled by train or plane. It may even have traveled by ship.

Have you ever thought about getting mail by horseback? There was a time when people living in the West got their mail this way. It was called the Pony Express. The Pony Express lasted less than two years. But, the skill and daring of its riders have become legendary in the American West.

Read the titles. Scan the texts. Look at the pictures and chart. ①

What do you think you will learn about **MAIL?**

The Original EXPRESS MAIL

④ Refer to the illustrations and photos to ask and answer questions about the texts.

Why do you think the Pony Express was used for only a short time?

VOCABULARY

legendary:
   describing something well known or made famous

motto:
   a brief statement used to express an idea or goal

relay:
   a series of persons taking turns

telegraph:
   a system for sending messages across distances by wires

transcontinental:
   crossing a continent

②

Americans were moving west in the mid-1800s. But, mail took a long time to reach them. They felt out of touch.

In 1860, the railroad and telegraph went only as far west as St. Joseph, Missouri. That was the year the Pony Express was born. St. Joseph was the starting point.

The Pony Express went between Missouri and California. Relay stations were set up every 10 to 15 miles (16 to 24 km). Riders rode 75 to 100 miles (121 to 161 km) a day. They changed horses at each relay station. The riders were very talented. A rider quickly draped the special mailbag over the new horse's saddle. Then, he jumped on and was off again! The riders covered 250 miles (402 km) each day. The first trip west took nine days and 23 hours. The first trip east took 11 days and 12 hours.

The transcontinental telegraph line was completed by October 1861. The Pony Express ended. But, it is still riding strong in the colorful history of the American West.

③ Read the texts. What questions do you have? Write them

• in the margins,
• in a notebook,
• or on self-stick notes.

Discuss the questions with others.

PONY EXPRESS STATIONS PER STATE*

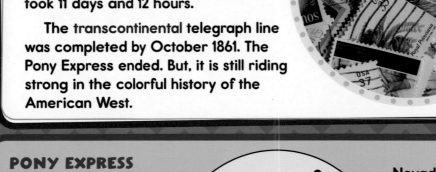

Nevada, 51
Utah, 26
Wyoming, 52
California, 18
Nebraska, 53
Kansas, 16
Colorado, 1
Missouri, 1

* Not all stations operated at the same time.

Have You Done This

PHILATELY?

Stamp collecting has been called "the hobby of kings and the king of hobbies." A king might call it *philately*. That's a fancy name for stamp collecting.

So, you're not royalty? That's OK. Stamp collecting still can be for you. It just takes the cost of a postage stamp to get started.

Sometimes, stamps are printed wrong. Printing mistakes are rare. But, they can make stamps valuable. The Inverted Jenny is a rare and valuable stamp. It shows an airplane that is upside down. It sold at an auction for $977,500!

Look closely the next time you get mail. You could have the next Inverted Jenny!

MAIL

Takes Flight

PAR AVION

AIRMAIL

Airplanes were used during World War I. Planes were very helpful to our military. They could deliver supplies to faraway places. So, it made sense that airplanes should be used to carry mail too.

The US Congress put aside some money in 1918. It was used to set up airmail routes. The first route was between New York City, New York and Washington, D.C. The route had one stop at Philadelphia, Pennsylvania. The first airmail trip took just over three hours. The delivery included a letter for the president.

"In rain or shine, snow or sleet, mail is delivered." This is a motto for mail carriers. But, the rain, snow, and sleet were problems for early airmail. Over time, these bumps in the sky were worked out. Airmail soon became a popular form of mail delivery.

WRITE ABOUT IT. ⑥
Imagine you received a letter from Brazil. What mail delivery system do you think was used? What makes you think so?

IT'S IN THE MAIL

How do you send mail? Do you click "send" to fire off an email? Or do you like to use snail mail?

Email lets people send notes around the world or around the corner very quickly. Some teachers use email to communicate with parents. Sorry, kids—no more notes getting lost in backpacks!

But, mail wasn't always as simple as sending an email. Have you ever received a card or letter in your mailbox? How did it get there? It may have traveled by truck. It may have traveled by train or plane. It may even have traveled by ship.

Have you ever thought about getting mail by horseback? There was a time when people living in the West got their mail this way. It was called the Pony Express. The Pony Express lasted less than two years. But, the skill and daring of its riders have become legendary in the American West.

Read the titles. Scan the texts. Look at the pictures and chart. ①

What do you think you will learn about MAIL?

The Original **EXPRESS MAIL**

④ Refer to the illustrations and photos to ask and answer questions about the texts.

Why do you think the Pony Express was used for only a short time?

VOCABULARY

legendary:
describing something well known or made famous

motto:
a brief statement used to express an idea or goal

relay:
a series of persons taking turns

telegraph:
a system for sending messages across distances by wires

transcontinental:
crossing a continent

②

Americans were moving west in the mid-1800s. But, mail took a long time to reach them. They felt out of touch.

In 1860, the railroad and telegraph went only as far west as St. Joseph, Missouri. That was the year the Pony Express was born. St. Joseph was the starting point.

The Pony Express went between Missouri and California. Relay stations were set up every 10 to 15 miles (16 to 24 km). Riders rode 75 to 100 miles (121 to 161 km) a day. They changed horses at each relay station. The riders were very talented. A rider quickly draped the special mailbag over the new horse's saddle. Then, he jumped on and was off again! The riders covered 250 miles (402 km) each day. The first trip west took nine days and 23 hours. The first trip east took 11 days and 12 hours.

The transcontinental telegraph line was completed by October 1861. The Pony Express ended. But, it is still riding strong in the colorful history of the American West.

Have You Done This

PHILATELY?

Stamp collecting has been called "the hobby of kings and the king of hobbies." A king might call it *philately*. That's a fancy name for stamp collecting.

So, you're not royalty? That's OK. Stamp collecting still can be for you. It just takes the cost of a postage stamp to get started.

Sometimes, stamps are printed wrong. Printing mistakes are rare. But, they can make stamps valuable. The Inverted Jenny is a rare and valuable stamp. It shows an airplane that is upside down. It sold at an auction for $977,500!

Look closely the next time you get mail. You could have the next Inverted Jenny!

Read the texts. What questions do you have? Write them

• in the margins,
• in a notebook,
• or on self-stick notes.

Discuss the questions with others.

③

PONY EXPRESS STATIONS PER STATE*

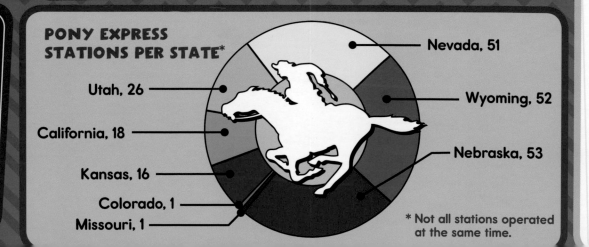

Nevada, 51

Utah, 26

Wyoming, 52

California, 18

Kansas, 16

Nebraska, 53

Colorado, 1

Missouri, 1

* Not all stations operated at the same time.

MAIL
Takes Flight

PAR AVION

AIRMAIL

Airplanes were used during World War I. Planes were very helpful to our military. They could deliver supplies to faraway places. So, it made sense that airplanes should be used to carry mail too.

The US Congress put aside some money in 1918. It was used to set up airmail routes. The first route was between New York City, New York and Washington, D.C. The route had one stop at Philadelphia, Pennsylvania. The first airmail trip took just over three hours. The delivery included a letter for the president.

"In rain or shine, snow or sleet, mail is delivered." This is a motto for mail carriers. But, the rain, snow, and sleet were problems for early airmail. Over time, these bumps in the sky were worked out. Airmail soon became a popular form of mail delivery.

WRITE ABOUT IT. ⑥
Imagine you received a letter from Brazil. What mail delivery system do you think was used? What makes you think so?

© Carson-Dellosa CD-104930

QUESTION to wonder about information in the text

IT'S IN THE MAIL

How do you send mail? Do you click "send" to fire off an email? Or do you like to use snail mail?

Email lets people send notes around the world or around the corner very quickly. Some teachers use email to communicate with parents. Sorry, kids—no more notes getting lost in backpacks!

But, mail wasn't always as simple as sending an email. Have you ever received a card or letter in your mailbox? How did it get there? It may have traveled by truck. It may have traveled by train or plane. It may even have traveled by ship.

Have you ever thought about getting mail by horseback? There was a time when people living in the West got their mail this way. It was called the Pony Express. The Pony Express lasted less than two years. But, the skill and daring of its riders have become legendary in the American West.

Read the titles. Scan the texts. Look at the pictures and chart. ①

What do you think you will learn about **MAIL?**

The Original EXPRESS MAIL

Americans were moving west in the mid-1800s. But, mail took a long time to reach them. They felt out of touch.

In 1860, the railroad and telegraph went only as far west as St. Joseph, Missouri. That was the year the Pony Express was born. St. Joseph was the starting point.

The Pony Express went between Missouri and California. Relay stations were set up every 10 to 15 miles (16 to 24 km). Riders rode 75 to 100 miles (121 to 161 km) a day. They changed horses at each relay station. The riders were very talented. A rider quickly draped the special mailbag over the new horse's saddle. Then, he jumped on and was off again! The riders covered 250 miles (402 km) each day. The first trip west took nine days and 23 hours. The first trip east took 11 days and 12 hours.

The transcontinental telegraph line was completed by October 1861. The Pony Express ended. But, it is still riding strong in the colorful history of the American West.

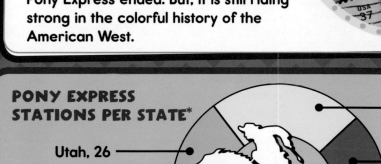

VOCABULARY

legendary:
describing something well known or made famous

motto:
a brief statement used to express an idea or goal

relay:
a series of persons taking turns

telegraph:
a system for sending messages across distances by wires

transcontinental:
crossing a continent

②

③ Read the texts. What questions do you have? Write them
- in the margins,
- in a notebook,
- or on self-stick notes.

Discuss the questions with others.

④ Refer to the illustrations and photos to ask and answer questions about the texts.

Why do you think the Pony Express was used for only a short time?

Have You Done This

PHILATELY?

Stamp collecting has been called "the hobby of kings and the king of hobbies." A king might call it *philately*. That's a fancy name for stamp collecting.

So, you're not royalty? That's OK. Stamp collecting still can be for you. It just takes the cost of a postage stamp to get started.

Sometimes, stamps are printed wrong. Printing mistakes are rare. But, they can make stamps valuable. The Inverted Jenny is a rare and valuable stamp. It shows an airplane that is upside down. It sold at an auction for $977,500!

Look closely the next time you get mail. You could have the next Inverted Jenny!

PONY EXPRESS STATIONS PER STATE*

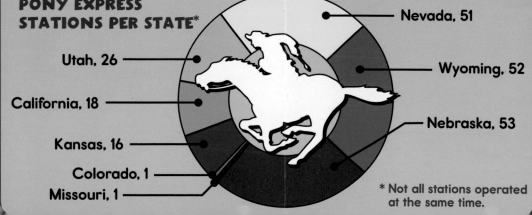

- Nevada, 51
- Utah, 26
- Wyoming, 52
- California, 18
- Nebraska, 53
- Kansas, 16
- Colorado, 1
- Missouri, 1

* Not all stations operated at the same time.

MAIL
Takes Flight

PAR AVION

AIRMAIL

Airplanes were used during World War I. Planes were very helpful to our military. They could deliver supplies to faraway places. So, it made sense that airplanes should be used to carry mail too.

The US Congress put aside some money in 1918. It was used to set up airmail routes. The first route was between New York City, New York and Washington, D.C. The route had one stop at Philadelphia, Pennsylvania. The first airmail trip took just over three hours. The delivery included a letter for the president.

"In rain or shine, snow or sleet, mail is delivered." This is a motto for mail carriers. But, the rain, snow, and sleet were problems for early airmail. Over time, these bumps in the sky were worked out. Airmail soon became a popular form of mail delivery.

WRITE ABOUT IT. ⑥
Imagine you received a letter from Brazil. What mail delivery system do you think was used? What makes you think so?

© Carson-Dellosa CD-104930

QUESTION to wonder about information in the text

IT'S IN THE MAIL

How do you send mail? Do you click "send" to fire off an email? Or do you like to use snail mail?

Email lets people send notes around the world or around the corner very quickly. Some teachers use email to communicate with parents. Sorry, kids—no more notes getting lost in backpacks!

But, mail wasn't always as simple as sending an email. Have you ever received a card or letter in your mailbox? How did it get there? It may have traveled by truck. It may have traveled by train or plane. It may even have traveled by ship.

Have you ever thought about getting mail by horseback? There was a time when people living in the West got their mail this way. It was called the Pony Express. The Pony Express lasted less than two years. But, the skill and daring of its riders have become legendary in the American West.

Read the titles. Scan the texts. Look at the pictures and chart. ①

What do you think you will learn about **MAIL?**

The Original EXPRESS MAIL

④ Refer to the illustrations and photos to ask and answer questions about the texts.

Why do you think the Pony Express was used for only a short time?

VOCABULARY

legendary:
describing something well known or made famous

motto:
a brief statement used to express an idea or goal

relay:
a series of persons taking turns

telegraph:
a system for sending messages across distances by wires

transcontinental:
crossing a continent

②

Americans were moving west in the mid-1800s. But, mail took a long time to reach them. They felt out of touch.

In 1860, the railroad and telegraph went only as far west as St. Joseph, Missouri. That was the year the Pony Express was born. St. Joseph was the starting point.

The Pony Express went between Missouri and California. Relay stations were set up every 10 to 15 miles (16 to 24 km). Riders rode 75 to 100 miles (121 to 161 km) a day. They changed horses at each relay station. The riders were very talented. A rider quickly draped the special mailbag over the new horse's saddle. Then, he jumped on and was off again! The riders covered 250 miles (402 km) each day. The first trip west took nine days and 23 hours. The first trip east took 11 days and 12 hours.

The transcontinental telegraph line was completed by October 1861. The Pony Express ended. But, it is still riding strong in the colorful history of the American West.

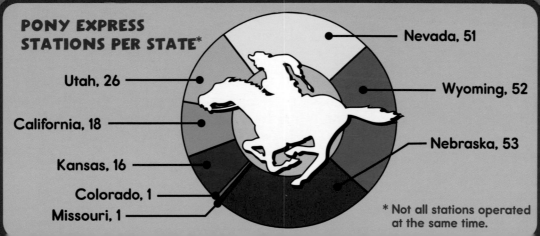

Have You Done This

PHILATELY?

Stamp collecting has been called "the hobby of kings and the king of hobbies." A king might call it *philately*. That's a fancy name for stamp collecting.

So, you're not royalty? That's OK. Stamp collecting still can be for you. It just takes the cost of a postage stamp to get started.

Sometimes, stamps are printed wrong. Printing mistakes are rare. But, they can make stamps valuable. The Inverted Jenny is a rare and valuable stamp. It shows an airplane that is upside down. It sold at an auction for $977,500!

Look closely the next time you get mail. You could have the next Inverted Jenny!

Read the texts. What questions do you have? Write them

• in the margins,
• in a notebook,
• or on self-stick notes.

Discuss the questions with others.

③

PONY EXPRESS STATIONS PER STATE*

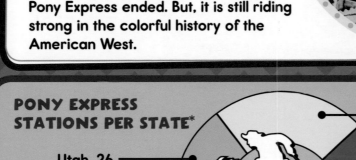

- Utah, 26
- California, 18
- Kansas, 16
- Colorado, 1
- Missouri, 1
- Nevada, 51
- Wyoming, 52
- Nebraska, 53

* Not all stations operated at the same time.

PAR AVION

MAIL
Takes Flight

AIRMAIL

Airplanes were used during World War I. Planes were very helpful to our military. They could deliver supplies to faraway places. So, it made sense that airplanes should be used to carry mail too.

The US Congress put aside some money in 1918. It was used to set up airmail routes. The first route was between New York City, New York and Washington, D.C. The route had one stop at Philadelphia, Pennsylvania. The first airmail trip took just over three hours. The delivery included a letter for the president.

"In rain or shine, snow or sleet, mail is delivered." This is a motto for mail carriers. But, the rain, snow, and sleet were problems for early airmail. Over time, these bumps in the sky were worked out. Airmail soon became a popular form of mail delivery.

© Carson-Dellosa CD-104930

IT'S IN THE MAIL

How do you send mail? Do you click "send" to fire off an email? Or do you like to use snail mail?

Email lets people send notes around the world or around the corner very quickly. Some teachers use email to communicate with parents. Sorry, kids—no more notes getting lost in backpacks!

But, mail wasn't always as simple as sending an email. Have you ever received a card or letter in your mailbox? How did it get there? It may have traveled by truck. It may have traveled by train or plane. It may even have traveled by ship.

Have you ever thought about getting mail by horseback? There was a time when people living in the West got their mail this way. It was called the Pony Express. The Pony Express lasted less than two years. But, the skill and daring of its riders have become legendary in the American West.

Read the titles. Scan the texts. Look at the pictures and chart. 1

What do you think you will learn about **MAIL?**

The Original EXPRESS MAIL

Americans were moving west in the mid-1800s. But, mail took a long time to reach them. They felt out of touch.

In 1860, the railroad and telegraph went only as far west as St. Joseph, Missouri. That was the year the Pony Express was born. St. Joseph was the starting point.

The Pony Express went between Missouri and California. Relay stations were set up every 10 to 15 miles (16 to 24 km). Riders rode 75 to 100 miles (121 to 161 km) a day. They changed horses at each relay station. The riders were very talented. A rider quickly draped the special mailbag over the new horse's saddle. Then, he jumped on and was off again! The riders covered 250 miles (402 km) each day. The first trip west took nine days and 23 hours. The first trip east took 11 days and 12 hours.

The transcontinental telegraph line was completed by October 1861. The Pony Express ended. But, it is still riding strong in the colorful history of the American West.

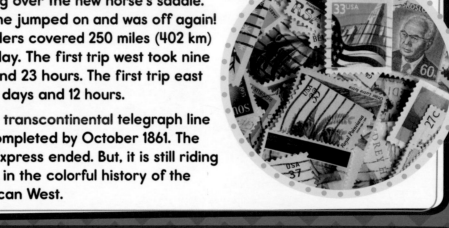

④ Refer to the illustrations and photos to ask and answer questions about the texts.

Why do you think the Pony Express was used for only a short time?

VOCABULARY

legendary:
describing something well known or made famous

motto:
a brief statement used to express an idea or goal

relay:
a series of persons taking turns

telegraph:
a system for sending messages across distances by wires

transcontinental:
crossing a continent

②

③ Read the texts. What questions do you have? Write them
- in the margins,
- in a notebook,
- or on self-stick notes.

Discuss the questions with others.

Have You Done This

PHILATELY?

Stamp collecting has been called "the hobby of kings and the king of hobbies." A king might call it *philately*. That's a fancy name for stamp collecting.

So, you're not royalty? That's OK. Stamp collecting still can be for you. It just takes the cost of a postage stamp to get started.

Sometimes, stamps are printed wrong. Printing mistakes are rare. But, they can make stamps valuable. The Inverted Jenny is a rare and valuable stamp. It shows an airplane that is upside down. It sold at an auction for $977,500!

Look closely the next time you get mail. You could have the next Inverted Jenny!

PONY EXPRESS STATIONS PER STATE*

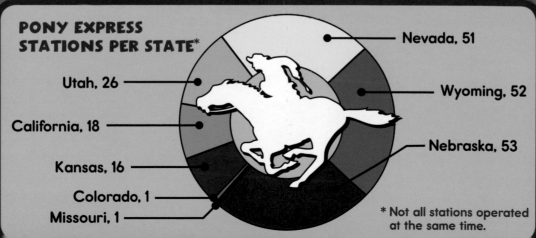

- Nevada, 51
- Utah, 26
- Wyoming, 52
- California, 18
- Nebraska, 53
- Kansas, 16
- Colorado, 1
- Missouri, 1

* Not all stations operated at the same time.

MAIL
Takes Flight

PAR AVION

AIRMAIL

Airplanes were used during World War I. Planes were very helpful to our military. They could deliver supplies to faraway places. So, it made sense that airplanes should be used to carry mail too.

The US Congress put aside some money in 1918. It was used to set up airmail routes. The first route was between New York City, New York and Washington, D.C. The route had one stop at Philadelphia, Pennsylvania. The first airmail trip took just over three hours. The delivery included a letter for the president.

"In rain or shine, snow or sleet, mail is delivered." This is a motto for mail carriers. But, the rain, snow, and sleet were problems for early airmail. Over time, these bumps in the sky were worked out. Airmail soon became a popular form of mail delivery.

WRITE ABOUT IT. ⑥
Imagine you received a letter from Brazil. What mail delivery system do you think was used? What makes you think so?

QUESTION to wonder
about information in the text

IT'S IN THE MAIL

How do you send mail? Do you click "send" to fire off an email? Or do you like to use snail mail?

Email lets people send notes around the world or around the corner very quickly. Some teachers use email to communicate with parents. Sorry, kids—no more notes getting lost in backpacks!

But, mail wasn't always as simple as sending an email. Have you ever received a card or letter in your mailbox? How did it get there? It may have traveled by truck. It may have traveled by train or plane. It may even have traveled by ship.

Have you ever thought about getting mail by horseback? There was a time when people living in the West got their mail this way. It was called the Pony Express. The Pony Express lasted less than two years. But, the skill and daring of its riders have become legendary in the American West.

① Read the titles. Scan the texts. Look at the pictures and chart.

What do you think you will learn about **MAIL?**

The Original EXPRESS MAIL

④ Refer to the illustrations and photos to ask and answer questions about the texts.

Why do you think the Pony Express was used for only a short time?

VOCABULARY

legendary:
describing something well known or made famous

motto:
a brief statement used to express an idea or goal

relay:
a series of persons taking turns

telegraph:
a system for sending messages across distances by wires

transcontinental:
crossing a continent

②

Americans were moving west in the mid-1800s. But, mail took a long time to reach them. They felt out of touch.

In 1860, the railroad and telegraph went only as far west as St. Joseph, Missouri. That was the year the Pony Express was born. St. Joseph was the starting point.

The Pony Express went between Missouri and California. Relay stations were set up every 10 to 15 miles (16 to 24 km). Riders rode 75 to 100 miles (121 to 161 km) a day. They changed horses at each relay station. The riders were very talented. A rider quickly draped the special mailbag over the new horse's saddle. Then, he jumped on and was off again! The riders covered 250 miles (402 km) each day. The first trip west took nine days and 23 hours. The first trip east took 11 days and 12 hours.

The transcontinental telegraph line was completed by October 1861. The Pony Express ended. But, it is still riding strong in the colorful history of the American West.

Read the texts. What questions do you have? Write them
- in the margins,
- in a notebook,
- or on self-stick notes.

Discuss the questions with others.

③

PONY EXPRESS STATIONS PER STATE*

- Nevada, 51
- Utah, 26
- Wyoming, 52
- California, 18
- Nebraska, 53
- Kansas, 16
- Colorado, 1
- Missouri, 1

* Not all stations operated at the same time.

Have You Done This

PHILATELY?

Stamp collecting has been called "the hobby of kings and the king of hobbies." A king might call it *philately*. That's a fancy name for stamp collecting.

So, you're not royalty? That's OK. Stamp collecting still can be for you. It just takes the cost of a postage stamp to get started.

Sometimes, stamps are printed wrong. Printing mistakes are rare. But, they can make stamps valuable. The Inverted Jenny is a rare and valuable stamp. It shows an airplane that is upside down. It sold at an auction for $977,500!

Look closely the next time you get mail. You could have the next Inverted Jenny!

READ THE TEXTS AGAIN. ⑤
Put the facts together. How does the author connect the texts?

GIRL POWER
Takes Flight

QUESTION to wonder about information in the text

Soaring into HISTORY

Have you ever seen six blue jets streaking through the sky? Those were the Blue Angels. The Blue Angels are the United States Navy's flight demonstration squad. Members of the Navy and Marines pilot them. Captain Katie Higgins is one of those pilots. She is the first female Blue Angel.

Captain Higgins has broken the sound barrier. But, she also broke the gender barrier. Katie Higgins knows she's making a difference. You can often find her at Blue Angels shows, meeting young girls. She tells them to go after their dreams. Captain Higgins says that we will have reached true equality when she is known not as the "Lady Blue Angel" but as just another pilot.

Amelia Earhart was 10 years old when she saw her first airplane. She was at a state fair. She was not impressed. It was a "thing of rusty wire and wood." Jump ahead 12 years. That same girl took her first plane ride. Earhart spent the rest of her life soaring into history.

Earhart got her international pilot's license at age 26. She was only the 16th woman to do so.

Earhart continued to set records. She set a women's world flying speed record. Later, she was the first woman to fly solo across the Atlantic. It's no surprise then that Earhart was the first person to fly solo across the Pacific Ocean from Hawaii to California.

Sadly, Earhart's biggest dream was never fulfilled. She wanted to become the first woman to fly around the world. But on July 2, 1937, her plane disappeared over the Pacific. Amelia Earhart was never heard from again.

Read the titles. Scan the texts. Look at the pictures and map. ①

What do you think you will learn about **FLYING?**

WRITE ABOUT IT. ⑥
Think about how pilots have changed through the years. What are the most important changes? Why?

The **MYSTERY** of Amelia Earhart

Refer to the illustrations and photos to answer questions you have about the texts.

4

How and why do you think Amelia Earhart made history?

VOCABULARY

air traffic controller:
  a person on the ground who gives instructions by radio to pilots

demonstration:
  the act of showing how something works

gender:
  male or female

sound barrier:
  a sudden increase in resistance that happens when an aircraft gets close to the speed of sound

2

Amelia Earhart was the queen of the air in the 1930s. And, she was about to make history again. She did, but not in the way she had hoped.

In June 1937, Amelia began her flight around the world. The first leg of the trip was a success. She made it to New Guinea in 29 days. Her next stop was to be a small island in the middle of the Pacific Ocean. But, she never made it there. July 2, 1937, was the last time Amelia was heard from. She, her navigator, and her plane vanished.

Many theories have emerged about what may have happened to Amelia Earhart. Was she a spy? Did enemies of the United States capture her? Did she get lost? Did she run out of fuel? Maybe you will be the one to finally solve the mystery of Amelia Earhart.

RADIO DETECTION AND RANGING

Why are some of the letters in the title BLUE? Look at only the blue letters. You will see where the word *radar* comes from. Radar has been around since the 1930s. It was invented to help the military. They used it to detect planes in the air.

Now, air traffic controllers and aircraft pilots use radar. At any given moment, more than 5,000 planes are in the sky above the United States. Radar is used so that planes can avoid each other.

Read the texts. What questions do you have? Write them

- in the margins,
- in a notebook,
- or on self-stick notes.

3

Discuss the questions with others.

THE MYSTERIOUS FINAL FLIGHT

Oakland, California
May 20

Miami, Florida
June 1

Assab, Eritrea
June 15

Bangkok, Thailand
June 20

Singapore
June 21

Caripito, Venezuela
June 3

Dakar, Senegal
June 10

Karachi, Pakistan
June 17

Natal, Brazil
June 7

Darwin, Australia
June 29

Lae, Papua New Guinea
July 2

GIRL POWER
Takes Flight

Have you ever seen six blue jets streaking through the sky? Those were the Blue Angels. The Blue Angels are the United States Navy's flight demonstration squad. Members of the Navy and Marines pilot them. Captain Katie Higgins is one of those pilots. She is the first female Blue Angel.

Captain Higgins has broken the sound barrier. But, she also broke the gender barrier. Katie Higgins knows she's making a difference. You can often find her at Blue Angels shows, meeting young girls. She tells them to go after their dreams. Captain Higgins says that we will have reached true equality when she is known not as the "Lady Blue Angel" but as just another pilot.

WRITE ABOUT IT. 6
Think about how pilots have changed through the years. What are the most important changes? Why?

QUESTION to wonder about information in the text

Soaring into HISTORY

Amelia Earhart was 10 years old when she saw her first airplane. She was at a state fair. She was not impressed. It was a "thing of rusty wire and wood." Jump ahead 12 years. That same girl took her first plane ride. Earhart spent the rest of her life soaring into history.

Earhart got her international pilot's license at age 26. She was only the 16th woman to do so.

Earhart continued to set records. She set a women's world flying speed record. Later, she was the first woman to fly solo across the Atlantic. It's no surprise then that Earhart was the first person to fly solo across the Pacific Ocean from Hawaii to California.

Sadly, Earhart's biggest dream was never fulfilled. She wanted to become the first woman to fly around the world. But on July 2, 1937, her plane disappeared over the Pacific. Amelia Earhart was never heard from again.

Read the titles. Scan the texts. Look at the pictures and map. 1

What do you think you will learn about **FLYING?**

The **MYSTERY** of Amelia Earhart

Refer to the illustrations and photos to answer questions you have about the texts.

4

How and why do you think Amelia Earhart made history?

VOCABULARY

air traffic controller:
a person on the ground who gives instructions by radio to pilots

demonstration:
the act of showing how something works

gender:
male or female

sound barrier:
a sudden increase in resistance that happens when an aircraft gets close to the speed of sound

2

Amelia Earhart was the queen of the air in the 1930s. And, she was about to make history again. She did, but not in the way she had hoped.

In June 1937, Amelia began her flight around the world. The first leg of the trip was a success. She made it to New Guinea in 29 days. Her next stop was to be a small island in the middle of the Pacific Ocean. But, she never made it there. July 2, 1937, was the last time Amelia was heard from. She, her navigator, and her plane vanished.

Many theories have emerged about what may have happened to Amelia Earhart. Was she a spy? Did enemies of the United States capture her? Did she get lost? Did she run out of fuel? Maybe you will be the one to finally solve the mystery of Amelia Earhart.

RADIO DETECTION AND RANGING

Why are some of the letters in the title **BLUE**? Look at only the blue letters. You will see where the word *radar* comes from. Radar has been around since the 1930s. It was invented to help the military. They used it to detect planes in the air.

Now, air traffic controllers and aircraft pilots use radar. At any given moment, more than 5,000 planes are in the sky above the United States. Radar is used so that planes can avoid each other.

Read the texts. What questions do you have? Write them

- in the margins,
- in a notebook,
- or on self-stick notes.

3

Discuss the questions with others.

THE MYSTERIOUS FINAL FLIGHT

Oakland, California
May 20

Miami, Florida
June 1

Assab, Eritrea
June 15

Bangkok, Thailand
June 20

Singapore
June 21

Caripito, Venezuela
June 3

Dakar, Senegal
June 10

Karachi, Pakistan
June 17

Lae, Papua New Guinea
July 2

Natal, Brazil
June 7

Darwin, Australia
June 29

READ THE TEXTS AGAIN. 5

Put the facts together. How does the author connect the texts?

GIRL POWER

Takes Flight

Have you ever seen six blue jets streaking through the sky? Those were the Blue Angels. The Blue Angels are the United States Navy's flight demonstration squad. Members of the Navy and Marines pilot them. Captain Katie Higgins is one of those pilots. She is the first female Blue Angel.

Captain Higgins has broken the sound barrier. But, she also broke the gender barrier. Katie Higgins knows she's making a difference. You can often find her at Blue Angels shows, meeting young girls. She tells them to go after their dreams. Captain Higgins says that we will have reached true equality when she is known not as the "Lady Blue Angel" but as just another pilot.

WRITE ABOUT IT. 6

Think about how pilots have changed through the years. What are the most important changes? Why?

© Carson-Dellosa CD-104930

QUESTION to wonder about information in the text

Soaring into HISTORY

Amelia Earhart was 10 years old when she saw her first airplane. She was at a state fair. She was not impressed. It was a "thing of rusty wire and wood." Jump ahead 12 years. That same girl took her first plane ride. Earhart spent the rest of her life soaring into history.

Earhart got her international pilot's license at age 26. She was only the 16th woman to do so.

Earhart continued to set records. She set a women's world flying speed record. Later, she was the first woman to fly solo across the Atlantic. It's no surprise then that Earhart was the first person to fly solo across the Pacific Ocean from Hawaii to California.

Sadly, Earhart's biggest dream was never fulfilled. She wanted to become the first woman to fly around the world. But on July 2, 1937, her plane disappeared over the Pacific. Amelia Earhart was never heard from again.

Read the titles. Scan the texts. Look at the pictures and map. 1

What do you think you will learn about **FLYING?**

The MYSTERY of Amelia Earhart

Refer to the illustrations and photos to answer questions you have about the texts.

④

How and why do you think Amelia Earhart made history?

Amelia Earhart was the queen of the air in the 1930s. And, she was about to make history again. She did, but not in the way she had hoped.

In June 1937, Amelia began her flight around the world. The first leg of the trip was a success. She made it to New Guinea in 29 days. Her next stop was to be a small island in the middle of the Pacific Ocean. But, she never made it there. July 2, 1937, was the last time Amelia was heard from. She, her navigator, and her plane vanished.

Many theories have emerged about what may have happened to Amelia Earhart. Was she a spy? Did enemies of the United States capture her? Did she get lost? Did she run out of fuel? Maybe you will be the one to finally solve the mystery of Amelia Earhart.

VOCABULARY

air traffic controller:
a person on the ground who gives instructions by radio to pilots

demonstration:
the act of showing how something works

gender:
male or female

sound barrier:
a sudden increase in resistance that happens when an aircraft gets close to the speed of sound

②

Read the texts. What questions do you have? Write them

• in the margins,
• in a notebook,
• or on self-stick notes.

③

Discuss the questions with others.

THE MYSTERIOUS FINAL FLIGHT

Oakland, California
May 20

Miami, Florida
June 1

Assab, Eritrea
June 15

Bangkok, Thailand
June 20

Caripito, Venezuela
June 3

Dakar, Senegal
June 10

Karachi,
Pakistan
June 17

Singapore
June 21

Natal, Brazil
June 7

Darwin,
Australia
June 29

Lae, Papua
New Guinea
July 2

?

RADIO DETECTION AND RANGING

Why are some of the letters in the title **BLUE**? Look at only the blue letters. You will see where the word *radar* comes from. Radar has been around since the 1930s. It was invented to help the military. They used it to detect planes in the air.

Now, air traffic controllers and aircraft pilots use radar. At any given moment, more than 5,000 planes are in the sky above the United States. Radar is used so that planes can avoid each other.

READE THE TEXTS AGAIN. 5
Put the facts together. How does the
author connect the texts?

GIRL POWER
Takes Flight

Soaring into HISTORY

Have you ever seen six blue jets streaking through the sky? Those were the Blue Angels. The Blue Angels are the United States Navy's flight demonstration squad. Members of the Navy and Marines pilot them. Captain Katie Higgins is one of those pilots. She is the first female Blue Angel.

Captain Higgins has broken the sound barrier. But, she also broke the gender barrier. Katie Higgins knows she's making a difference. You can often find her at Blue Angels shows, meeting young girls. She tells them to go after their dreams. Captain Higgins says that we will have reached true equality when she is known not as the "Lady Blue Angel" but as just another pilot.

Amelia Earhart was 10 years old when she saw her first airplane. She was at a state fair. She was not impressed. It was a "thing of rusty wire and wood." Jump ahead 12 years. That same girl took her first plane ride. Earhart spent the rest of her life soaring into history.

Earhart got her international pilot's license at age 26. She was only the 16th woman to do so.

Earhart continued to set records. She set a women's world flying speed record. Later, she was the first woman to fly solo across the Atlantic. It's no surprise then that Earhart was the first person to fly solo across the Pacific Ocean from Hawaii to California.

Sadly, Earhart's biggest dream was never fulfilled. She wanted to become the first woman to fly around the world. But on July 2, 1937, her plane disappeared over the Pacific. Amelia Earhart was never heard from again.

Read the titles. Scan the texts. Look at the pictures and map. 1

What do you think you will learn about **FLYING?**

WRITE ABOUT IT. 6
Think about how pilots have changed through the years. What are the most important changes? Why?

The MYSTERY of Amelia Earhart

Refer to the illustrations and photos to answer questions you have about the texts.

4

How and why do you think Amelia Earhart made history?

VOCABULARY

air traffic controller:
a person on the ground who gives instructions by radio to pilots

demonstration:
the act of showing how something works

gender:
male or female

sound barrier:
a sudden increase in resistance that happens when an aircraft gets close to the speed of sound

2

Amelia Earhart was the queen of the air in the 1930s. And, she was about to make history again. She did, but not in the way she had hoped.

In June 1937, Amelia began her flight around the world. The first leg of the trip was a success. She made it to New Guinea in 29 days. Her next stop was to be a small island in the middle of the Pacific Ocean. But, she never made it there. July 2, 1937, was the last time Amelia was heard from. She, her navigator, and her plane vanished.

Many theories have emerged about what may have happened to Amelia Earhart. Was she a spy? Did enemies of the United States capture her? Did she get lost? Did she run out of fuel? Maybe you will be the one to finally solve the mystery of Amelia Earhart.

Read the texts. What questions do you have? Write them
- in the margins,
- in a notebook,
- or on self-stick notes.

3

Discuss the questions with others.

RADIO DETECTION AND RANGING

Why are some of the letters in the title **BLUE**? Look at only the blue letters. You will see where the word *radar* comes from. Radar has been around since the 1930s. It was invented to help the military. They used it to detect planes in the air.

Now, air traffic controllers and aircraft pilots use radar. At any given moment, more than 5,000 planes are in the sky above the United States. Radar is used so that planes can avoid each other.

THE MYSTERIOUS FINAL FLIGHT

Oakland, California
May 20

Miami, Florida
June 1

Assab, Eritrea
June 15

Bangkok, Thailand
June 20

Caripito, Venezuela
June 3

Dakar, Senegal
June 10

Karachi, Pakistan
June 17

Singapore
June 21

Natal, Brazil
June 7

Darwin, Australia
June 29

Lae, Papua New Guinea
July 2

?

READE THE TEXTS AGAIN. ⑤

Put the facts together. How does the author connect the texts?

GIRL POWER
Takes Flight

Have you ever seen six blue jets streaking through the sky? Those were the Blue Angels. The Blue Angels are the United States Navy's flight demonstration squad. Members of the Navy and Marines pilot them. Captain Katie Higgins is one of those pilots. She is the first female Blue Angel.

Captain Higgins has broken the sound barrier. But, she also broke the gender barrier. Katie Higgins knows she's making a difference. You can often find her at Blue Angels shows, meeting young girls. She tells them to go after their dreams. Captain Higgins says that we will have reached true equality when she is known not as the "Lady Blue Angel" but as just another pilot.

WRITE ABOUT IT. ⑥

Think about how pilots have changed through the years. What are the most important changes? Why?

QUESTION to wonder about information in the text

Soaring into HISTORY

Amelia Earhart was 10 years old when she saw her first airplane. She was at a state fair. She was not impressed. It was a "thing of rusty wire and wood." Jump ahead 12 years. That same girl took her first plane ride. Earhart spent the rest of her life soaring into history.

Earhart got her international pilot's license at age 26. She was only the 16th woman to do so.

Earhart continued to set records. She set a women's world flying speed record. Later, she was the first woman to fly solo across the Atlantic. It's no surprise then that Earhart was the first person to fly solo across the Pacific Ocean from Hawaii to California.

Sadly, Earhart's biggest dream was never fulfilled. She wanted to become the first woman to fly around the world. But on July 2, 1937, her plane disappeared over the Pacific. Amelia Earhart was never heard from again.

Read the titles. Scan the texts. Look at the pictures and map. ①

What do you think you will learn about **FLYING?**

The MYSTERY of Amelia Earhart

Refer to the illustrations and photos to answer questions you have about the texts.

④

How and why do you think Amelia Earhart made history?

VOCABULARY

air traffic controller:
a person on the ground who gives instructions by radio to pilots

demonstration:
the act of showing how something works

gender:
male or female

sound barrier:
a sudden increase in resistance that happens when an aircraft gets close to the speed of sound

②

Amelia Earhart was the queen of the air in the 1930s. And, she was about to make history again. She did, but not in the way she had hoped.

In June 1937, Amelia began her flight around the world. The first leg of the trip was a success. She made it to New Guinea in 29 days. Her next stop was to be a small island in the middle of the Pacific Ocean. But, she never made it there. July 2, 1937, was the last time Amelia was heard from. She, her navigator, and her plane vanished.

Many theories have emerged about what may have happened to Amelia Earhart. Was she a spy? Did enemies of the United States capture her? Did she get lost? Did she run out of fuel? Maybe you will be the one to finally solve the mystery of Amelia Earhart.

RADIO DETECTION AND RANGING

Why are some of the letters in the title **BLUE**? Look at only the blue letters. You will see where the word *radar* comes from. Radar has been around since the 1930s. It was invented to help the military. They used it to detect planes in the air.

Now, air traffic controllers and aircraft pilots use radar. At any given moment, more than 5,000 planes are in the sky above the United States. Radar is used so that planes can avoid each other.

Read the texts. What questions do you have? Write them

- in the margins,
- in a notebook,
- or on self-stick notes.

③

Discuss the questions with others.

THE MYSTERIOUS FINAL FLIGHT

Oakland, California
May 20

Miami, Florida
June 1

Assab, Eritrea
June 15

Bangkok, Thailand
June 20

Singapore
June 21

Caripito, Venezuela
June 3

Dakar, Senegal
June 10

Karachi, Pakistan
June 17

Natal, Brazil
June 7

Darwin, Australia
June 29

Lae, Papua New Guinea
July 2

?

READ THE TEXTS AGAIN. 5
Put the facts together. How does the author connect the texts?

GIRL POWER
Takes Flight

Have you ever seen six blue jets streaking through the sky? Those were the Blue Angels. The Blue Angels are the United States Navy's flight demonstration squad. Members of the Navy and Marines pilot them. Captain Katie Higgins is one of those pilots. She is the first female Blue Angel.

Captain Higgins has broken the sound barrier. But, she also broke the gender barrier. Katie Higgins knows she's making a difference. You can often find her at Blue Angels shows, meeting young girls. She tells them to go after their dreams. Captain Higgins says that we will have reached true equality when she is known not as the "Lady Blue Angel" but as just another pilot.

WRITE ABOUT IT. 6
Think about how pilots have changed through the years. What are the most important changes? Why?

© Carson-Dellosa CD-104930

QUESTION to wonder
about information in the text

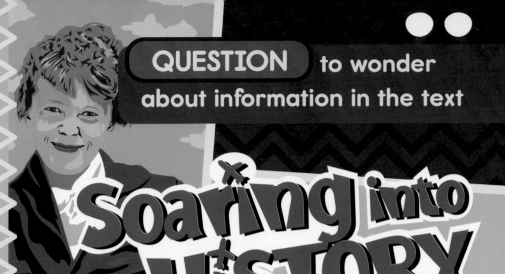

Soaring into HISTORY

Amelia Earhart was 10 years old when she saw her first airplane. She was at a state fair. She was not impressed. It was a "thing of rusty wire and wood." Jump ahead 12 years. That same girl took her first plane ride. Earhart spent the rest of her life soaring into history.

Earhart got her international pilot's license at age 26. She was only the 16th woman to do so.

Earhart continued to set records. She set a women's world flying speed record. Later, she was the first woman to fly solo across the Atlantic. It's no surprise then that Earhart was the first person to fly solo across the Pacific Ocean from Hawaii to California.

Sadly, Earhart's biggest dream was never fulfilled. She wanted to become the first woman to fly around the world. But on July 2, 1937, her plane disappeared over the Pacific. Amelia Earhart was never heard from again.

Read the titles. Scan the texts. Look at the pictures and map. 1

What do you think you will learn about FLYING?

The MYSTERY of Amelia Earhart

Refer to the illustrations and photos to answer questions you have about the texts.

④

How and why do you think Amelia Earhart made history?

VOCABULARY

air traffic controller:
a person on the ground who gives instructions by radio to pilots

demonstration:
the act of showing how something works

gender:
male or female

sound barrier:
a sudden increase in resistance that happens when an aircraft gets close to the speed of sound

②

Amelia Earhart was the queen of the air in the 1930s. And, she was about to make history again. She did, but not in the way she had hoped.

In June 1937, Amelia began her flight around the world. The first leg of the trip was a success. She made it to New Guinea in 29 days. Her next stop was to be a small island in the middle of the Pacific Ocean. But, she never made it there. July 2, 1937, was the last time Amelia was heard from. She, her navigator, and her plane vanished.

Many theories have emerged about what may have happened to Amelia Earhart. Was she a spy? Did enemies of the United States capture her? Did she get lost? Did she run out of fuel? Maybe you will be the one to finally solve the mystery of Amelia Earhart.

Read the texts. What questions do you have? Write them

- in the margins,
- in a notebook,
- or on self-stick notes.

③

Discuss the questions with others.

THE MYSTERIOUS FINAL FLIGHT

Oakland, California
May 20

Miami, Florida
June 1

Caripito, Venezuela
June 3

Natal, Brazil
June 7

Dakar, Senegal
June 10

Assab, Eritrea
June 15

Karachi, Pakistan
June 17

Bangkok, Thailand
June 20

Singapore
June 21

Darwin, Australia
June 29

Lae, Papua New Guinea
July 2

?

RADIO DETECTION AND RANGING

Why are some of the letters in the title **BLUE**? Look at only the blue letters. You will see where the word *radar* comes from. Radar has been around since the 1930s. It was invented to help the military. They used it to detect planes in the air.

Now, air traffic controllers and aircraft pilots use radar. At any given moment, more than 5,000 planes are in the sky above the United States. Radar is used so that planes can avoid each other.

THE GREATER
Good

Ben Franklin believed that people working together could accomplish great things. He always thought about the "greater good." He wanted to make people's lives better. Here are just a few of the ways he did just that.

- He started America's first lending library.
- He experimented with electricity.
- He signed the Declaration of Independence.
- He signed the US Constitution.
- He promoted abolishing slavery.
- He invented swim fins for hands.
- He invented an extension arm to reach books on high shelves.
- He greatly improved streetlights.
- He invented an odometer for a carriage.
- He organized a volunteer fire department.

WRITE ABOUT IT. (6)
What do you think is Benjamin Franklin's most important contribution? Why?

AMERICA'S GRANDFATHER

You know that George Washington is the Father of His Country, the United States of America. Then, Benjamin Franklin must surely be the Grandfather!

Franklin was a statesman. He signed the Declaration of Independence and the Constitution. He contributed to winning the Revolutionary War.

Franklin was an author and editor. He owned a newspaper called *The Pennsylvania Gazette*. People throughout the colonies read it. Franklin also wrote *Poor Richard's Almanack*. He published it for 25 years.

Franklin was a public servant. He became postmaster of Philadelphia in 1737. He founded a hospital. He organized a fire department. And, you can thank Ben Franklin the next time you visit a public library. He started America's first lending library.

Additionally, Franklin was an inventor. It is amazing how good your life is today because of many of Franklin's inventions.

Is it any wonder that Franklin is pictured on the US $100 bill?

Read the titles. Scan the texts. Look at the pictures and diagram. (1)

How did **BENJAMIN FRANKLIN** make lives better?

The TALENTED Mr. Franklin

Refer to the illustrations and photos to help you answer questions about the texts.

④ Why do you think Benjamin Franklin is an important figure in United States history?

VOCABULARY

extension:
something that is added to make an item longer

odometer:
instrument for measuring the distance traveled by a vehicle

patent:
to obtain the exclusive right to make or sell an invention

profit:
to make money

publish:
to prepare a written piece for public sale

②

③ Read the texts. What questions do you have? Write them
- in the margins,
- in a notebook,
- or on self-stick notes.

Discuss the questions with others.

Did you know that Benjamin Franklin did not patent any of his inventions? He did not profit from them, either. He invented them to make people's lives better.

In colonial times, homes used fireplaces for warmth. Franklin worked with a friend to invent a stove to replace the fireplace. Another inventor then improved the stove's design. The Franklin stove had much better airflow than a fireplace. It gave off more heat and less smoke. It also used less wood. The stove absorbed heat. This warmed the room long after the fire went out.

Franklin invented bifocals. He called them "double spectacles." The top half helped people see objects in the distance. The bottom half helped them see objects up close.

What would we do without electricity? Franklin did not invent electricity. But, he discovered many things about it. Because of his experiments, we can better understand it.

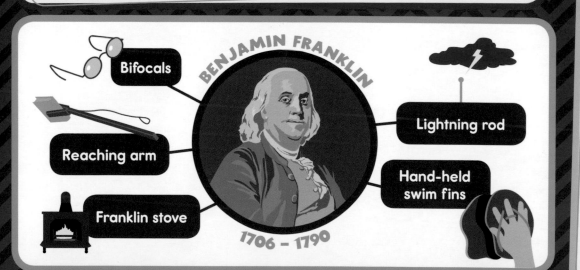

BENJAMIN FRANKLIN
1706 – 1790

- Bifocals
- Reaching arm
- Franklin stove
- Lightning rod
- Hand-held swim fins

BEN'S Shocking Invention

Franklin understood how electricity works. He wanted to figure out a way to protect houses from lightning. (Remember that then, most homes were made of wood. They caught fire easily if struck by lightning.)

The lightning rod is very simple. It is a metal rod attached to the top of a building. It is connected to the ground through a wire. The electric charge from the lightning strikes the rod. The charge follows the wire into the ground without harming the house or the people in it.

READ THE TEXTS AGAIN.
Put the facts together. What does the author want you to know about Benjamin Franklin?

5

THE GREATER Good

Ben Franklin believed that people working together could accomplish great things. He always thought about the "greater good." He wanted to make people's lives better. Here are just a few of the ways he did just that.

- He started America's first lending library.
- He experimented with electricity.
- He signed the Declaration of Independence.
- He signed the US Constitution.
- He promoted abolishing slavery.
- He invented swim fins for hands.
- He invented an extension arm to reach books on high shelves.
- He greatly improved streetlights.
- He invented an odometer for a carriage.
- He organized a volunteer fire department.

WRITE ABOUT IT.
What do you think is Benjamin Franklin's most important contribution? Why?

6

AMERICA'S GRANDFATHER

You know that George Washington is the Father of His Country, the United States of America. Then, Benjamin Franklin must surely be the Grandfather!

Franklin was a statesman. He signed the Declaration of Independence and the Constitution. He contributed to winning the Revolutionary War.

Franklin was an author and editor. He owned a newspaper called *The Pennsylvania Gazette*. People throughout the colonies read it. Franklin also wrote *Poor Richard's Almanack*. He published it for 25 years.

Franklin was a public servant. He became postmaster of Philadelphia in 1737. He founded a hospital. He organized a fire department. And, you can thank Ben Franklin the next time you visit a public library. He started America's first lending library.

Additionally, Franklin was an inventor. It is amazing how good your life is today because of many of Franklin's inventions.

Is it any wonder that Franklin is pictured on the US $100 bill?

Read the titles. Scan the texts. Look at the pictures and diagram.

1

How did **BENJAMIN FRANKLIN** make lives better?

The TALENTED Mr. Franklin

Refer to the illustrations and photos to help you answer questions about the texts.

Why do you think Benjamin Franklin is an important figure in United States history?

④

VOCABULARY

extension:
something that is added to make an item longer

odometer:
instrument for measuring the distance traveled by a vehicle

patent:
to obtain the exclusive right to make or sell an invention

profit:
to make money

publish:
to prepare a written piece for public sale

②

Did you know that Benjamin Franklin did not patent any of his inventions? He did not profit from them, either. He invented them to make people's lives better.

In colonial times, homes used fireplaces for warmth. Franklin worked with a friend to invent a stove to replace the fireplace. Another inventor then improved the stove's design. The Franklin stove had much better airflow than a fireplace. It gave off more heat and less smoke. It also used less wood. The stove absorbed heat. This warmed the room long after the fire went out.

Franklin invented bifocals. He called them "double spectacles." The top half helped people see objects in the distance. The bottom half helped them see objects up close.

What would we do without electricity? Franklin did not invent electricity. But, he discovered many things about it. Because of his experiments, we can better understand it.

BEN'S Shocking Invention

Franklin understood how electricity works. He wanted to figure out a way to protect houses from lightning. (Remember that then, most homes were made of wood. They caught fire easily if struck by lightning.)

The lightning rod is very simple. It is a metal rod attached to the top of a building. It is connected to the ground through a wire. The electric charge from the lightning strikes the rod. The charge follows the wire into the ground without harming the house or the people in it.

Read the texts. What questions do you have? Write them

- in the margins,
- in a notebook,
- or on self-stick notes.

Discuss the questions with others.

③

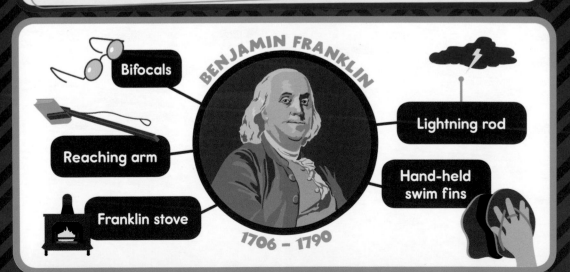

Bifocals
Reaching arm
Franklin stove
BENJAMIN FRANKLIN
Lightning rod
Hand-held swim fins
1706 – 1790

READ THE TEXTS AGAIN.
Put the facts together. What does the author want you to know about Benjamin Franklin?

5

THE GREATER
Good

Ben Franklin believed that people working together could accomplish great things. He always thought about the "greater good." He wanted to make people's lives better. Here are just a few of the ways he did just that.

- He started America's first lending library.
- He experimented with electricity.
- He signed the Declaration of Independence.
- He signed the US Constitution.
- He promoted abolishing slavery.
- He invented swim fins for hands.

- He invented an extension arm to reach books on high shelves.
- He greatly improved streetlights.
- He invented an odometer for a carriage.
- He organized a volunteer fire department.

WRITE ABOUT IT.
What do you think is Benjamin Franklin's most important contribution? Why?

6

AMERICA'S ★★★★★★ GRANDFATHER

You know that George Washington is the Father of His Country, the United States of America. Then, Benjamin Franklin must surely be the Grandfather!

Franklin was a statesman. He signed the Declaration of Independence and the Constitution. He contributed to winning the Revolutionary War.

Franklin was an author and editor. He owned a newspaper called *The Pennsylvania Gazette*. People throughout the colonies read it. Franklin also wrote *Poor Richard's Almanack*. He published it for 25 years.

Franklin was a public servant. He became postmaster of Philadelphia in 1737. He founded a hospital. He organized a fire department. And, you can thank Ben Franklin the next time you visit a public library. He started America's first lending library.

Additionally, Franklin was an inventor. It is amazing how good your life is today because of many of Franklin's inventions.

Is it any wonder that Franklin is pictured on the US $100 bill?

Read the titles. Scan the texts. Look at the pictures and diagram.

1

How did **BENJAMIN FRANKLIN** make lives better?

The TALENTED Mr. Franklin

Refer to the illustrations and photos to help you answer questions about the texts.

Why do you think Benjamin Franklin is an important figure in United States history?

④

VOCABULARY

extension:
something that is added to make an item longer

odometer:
instrument for measuring the distance traveled by a vehicle

patent:
to obtain the exclusive right to make or sell an invention

profit:
to make money

publish:
to prepare a written piece for public sale

②

Read the texts. What questions do you have? Write them

• in the margins,
• in a notebook,
• or on self-stick notes.

Discuss the questions with others.

③

Did you know that Benjamin Franklin did not patent any of his inventions? He did not profit from them, either. He invented them to make people's lives better.

In colonial times, homes used fireplaces for warmth. Franklin worked with a friend to invent a stove to replace the fireplace. Another inventor then improved the stove's design. The Franklin stove had much better airflow than a fireplace. It gave off more heat and less smoke. It also used less wood. The stove absorbed heat. This warmed the room long after the fire went out.

Franklin invented bifocals. He called them "double spectacles." The top half helped people see objects in the distance. The bottom half helped them see objects up close.

What would we do without electricity? Franklin did not invent electricity. But, he discovered many things about it. Because of his experiments, we can better understand it.

BEN'S
Shocking Invention

Franklin understood how electricity works. He wanted to figure out a way to protect houses from lightning. (Remember that then, most homes were made of wood. They caught fire easily if struck by lightning.)

The lightning rod is very simple. It is a metal rod attached to the top of a building. It is connected to the ground through a wire. The electric charge from the lightning strikes the rod. The charge follows the wire into the ground without harming the house or the people in it.

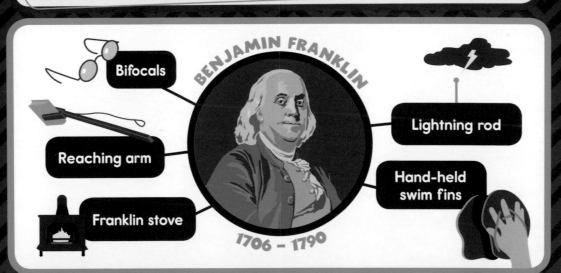

Bifocals
Reaching arm
Franklin stove
Lightning rod
Hand-held swim fins
BENJAMIN FRANKLIN
1706 – 1790

THE GREATER Good

Ben Franklin believed that people working together could accomplish great things. He always thought about the "greater good." He wanted to make people's lives better. Here are just a few of the ways he did just that.

- He started America's first lending library.
- He experimented with electricity.
- He signed the Declaration of Independence.
- He signed the US Constitution.
- He promoted abolishing slavery.
- He invented swim fins for hands.
- He invented an extension arm to reach books on high shelves.
- He greatly improved streetlights.
- He invented an odometer for a carriage.
- He organized a volunteer fire department.

AMERICA'S GRANDFATHER

You know that George Washington is the Father of His Country, the United States of America. Then, Benjamin Franklin must surely be the Grandfather!

Franklin was a statesman. He signed the Declaration of Independence and the Constitution. He contributed to winning the Revolutionary War.

Franklin was an author and editor. He owned a newspaper called *The Pennsylvania Gazette*. People throughout the colonies read it. Franklin also wrote *Poor Richard's Almanack*. He published it for 25 years.

Franklin was a public servant. He became postmaster of Philadelphia in 1737. He founded a hospital. He organized a fire department. And, you can thank Ben Franklin the next time you visit a public library. He started America's first lending library.

Additionally, Franklin was an inventor. It is amazing how good your life is today because of many of Franklin's inventions.

Is it any wonder that Franklin is pictured on the US $100 bill?

Read the titles. Scan the texts. Look at the pictures and diagram. ①

How did **BENJAMIN FRANKLIN** make lives better?

The TALENTED Mr. Franklin

④ Refer to the illustrations and photos to help you answer questions about the texts.

Why do you think Benjamin Franklin is an important figure in United States history?

VOCABULARY

extension:
something that is added to make an item longer

odometer:
instrument for measuring the distance traveled by a vehicle

patent:
to obtain the exclusive right to make or sell an invention

profit:
to make money

publish:
to prepare a written piece for public sale

②

Did you know that Benjamin Franklin did not patent any of his inventions? He did not profit from them, either. He invented them to make people's lives better.

In colonial times, homes used fireplaces for warmth. Franklin worked with a friend to invent a stove to replace the fireplace. Another inventor then improved the stove's design. The Franklin stove had much better airflow than a fireplace. It gave off more heat and less smoke. It also used less wood. The stove absorbed heat. This warmed the room long after the fire went out.

Franklin invented bifocals. He called them "double spectacles." The top half helped people see objects in the distance. The bottom half helped them see objects up close.

What would we do without electricity? Franklin did not invent electricity. But, he discovered many things about it. Because of his experiments, we can better understand it.

③ Read the texts. What questions do you have? Write them
- in the margins,
- in a notebook,
- or on self-stick notes.

Discuss the questions with others.

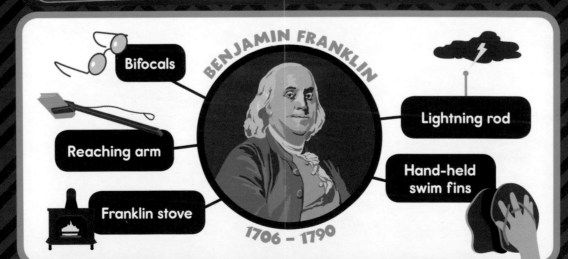

BENJAMIN FRANKLIN
- Bifocals
- Reaching arm
- Franklin stove
- Lightning rod
- Hand-held swim fins

1706 – 1790

BEN'S Shocking Invention

Franklin understood how electricity works. He wanted to figure out a way to protect houses from lightning. (Remember that then, most homes were made of wood. They caught fire easily if struck by lightning.)

The lightning rod is very simple. It is a metal rod attached to the top of a building. It is connected to the ground through a wire. The electric charge from the lightning strikes the rod. The charge follows the wire into the ground without harming the house or the people in it.

THE GREATER Good

Ben Franklin believed that people working together could accomplish great things. He always thought about the "greater good." He wanted to make people's lives better. Here are just a few of the ways he did just that.

-  He started America's first lending library.
- 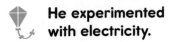 He experimented with electricity.
- He signed the Declaration of Independence.
- He signed the US Constitution.
- He promoted abolishing slavery.
- He invented swim fins for hands.

- He invented an extension arm to reach books on high shelves.
- He greatly improved streetlights.
- He invented an odometer for a carriage.
- He organized a volunteer fire department.

AMERICA'S GRANDFATHER

You know that George Washington is the Father of His Country, the United States of America. Then, Benjamin Franklin must surely be the Grandfather!

Franklin was a statesman. He signed the Declaration of Independence and the Constitution. He contributed to winning the Revolutionary War.

Franklin was an author and editor. He owned a newspaper called *The Pennsylvania Gazette*. People throughout the colonies read it. Franklin also wrote *Poor Richard's Almanack*. He published it for 25 years.

Franklin was a public servant. He became postmaster of Philadelphia in 1737. He founded a hospital. He organized a fire department. And, you can thank Ben Franklin the next time you visit a public library. He started America's first lending library.

Additionally, Franklin was an inventor. It is amazing how good your life is today because of many of Franklin's inventions.

Is it any wonder that Franklin is pictured on the US $100 bill?

Read the titles. Scan the texts. Look at the pictures and diagram. (1)

How did **BENJAMIN FRANKLIN** make lives better?

The TALENTED Mr. Franklin

④ Refer to the illustrations and photos to help you answer questions about the texts.

Why do you think Benjamin Franklin is an important figure in United States history?

VOCABULARY

extension:
: something that is added to make an item longer

odometer:
: instrument for measuring the distance traveled by a vehicle

patent:
: to obtain the exclusive right to make or sell an invention

profit:
: to make money

publish:
: to prepare a written piece for public sale

② Did you know that Benjamin Franklin did not patent any of his inventions? He did not profit from them, either. He invented them to make people's lives better.

In colonial times, homes used fireplaces for warmth. Franklin worked with a friend to invent a stove to replace the fireplace. Another inventor then improved the stove's design. The Franklin stove had much better airflow than a fireplace. It gave off more heat and less smoke. It also used less wood. The stove absorbed heat. This warmed the room long after the fire went out.

Franklin invented bifocals. He called them "double spectacles." The top half helped people see objects in the distance. The bottom half helped them see objects up close.

What would we do without electricity? Franklin did not invent electricity. But, he discovered many things about it. Because of his experiments, we can better understand it.

③ Read the texts. What questions do you have? Write them

• in the margins,
• in a notebook,
• or on self-stick notes.

Discuss the questions with others.

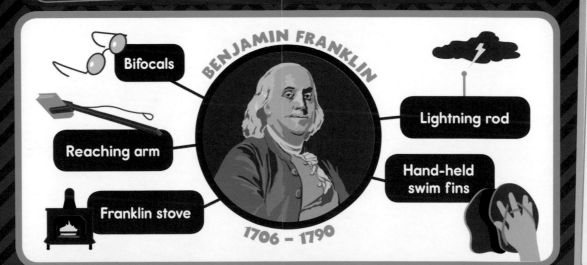

BENJAMIN FRANKLIN
1706 – 1790

Bifocals · Reaching arm · Franklin stove · Lightning rod · Hand-held swim fins

BEN'S Shocking Invention

Franklin understood how electricity works. He wanted to figure out a way to protect houses from lightning. (Remember that then, most homes were made of wood. They caught fire easily if struck by lightning.)

The lightning rod is very simple. It is a metal rod attached to the top of a building. It is connected to the ground through a wire. The electric charge from the lightning strikes the rod. The charge follows the wire into the ground without harming the house or the people in it.

THE GREATER
Good

Ben Franklin believed that people working together could accomplish great things. He always thought about the "greater good." He wanted to make people's lives better. Here are just a few of the ways he did just that.

 He started America's first lending library.

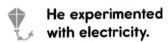 He experimented with electricity.

He signed the Declaration of Independence.

He signed the US Constitution.

He promoted abolishing slavery.

He invented swim fins for hands.

He invented an extension arm to reach books on high shelves.

He greatly improved streetlights.

He invented an odometer for a carriage.

He organized a volunteer fire department.

WRITE ABOUT IT. ⑥
What do you think is Benjamin Franklin's most important contribution? Why?

© Carson-Dellosa CD-104930

AMERICA'S GRANDFATHER

You know that George Washington is the Father of His Country, the United States of America. Then, Benjamin Franklin must surely be the Grandfather!

Franklin was a statesman. He signed the Declaration of Independence and the Constitution. He contributed to winning the Revolutionary War.

Franklin was an author and editor. He owned a newspaper called *The Pennsylvania Gazette*. People throughout the colonies read it. Franklin also wrote *Poor Richard's Almanack*. He published it for 25 years.

Franklin was a public servant. He became postmaster of Philadelphia in 1737. He founded a hospital. He organized a fire department. And, you can thank Ben Franklin the next time you visit a public library. He started America's first lending library.

Additionally, Franklin was an inventor. It is amazing how good your life is today because of many of Franklin's inventions.

Is it any wonder that Franklin is pictured on the US $100 bill?

Read the titles. Scan the texts. Look at the pictures and diagram. ①

How did **BENJAMIN FRANKLIN** make lives better?

The TALENTED Mr. Franklin

Refer to the illustrations and photos to help you answer questions about the texts.

4 Why do you think Benjamin Franklin is an important figure in United States history?

VOCABULARY

extension:
something that is added to make an item longer

odometer:
instrument for measuring the distance traveled by a vehicle

patent:
to obtain the exclusive right to make or sell an invention

profit:
to make money

publish:
to prepare a written piece for public sale

2

Did you know that Benjamin Franklin did not patent any of his inventions? He did not profit from them, either. He invented them to make people's lives better.

In colonial times, homes used fireplaces for warmth. Franklin worked with a friend to invent a stove to replace the fireplace. Another inventor then improved the stove's design. The Franklin stove had much better airflow than a fireplace. It gave off more heat and less smoke. It also used less wood. The stove absorbed heat. This warmed the room long after the fire went out.

Franklin invented bifocals. He called them "double spectacles." The top half helped people see objects in the distance. The bottom half helped them see objects up close.

What would we do without electricity? Franklin did not invent electricity. But, he discovered many things about it. Because of his experiments, we can better understand it.

3

Read the texts. What questions do you have? Write them

- in the margins,
- in a notebook,
- or on self-stick notes.

Discuss the questions with others.

BENJAMIN FRANKLIN

Bifocals

Reaching arm

Franklin stove

Lightning rod

Hand-held swim fins

1706 – 1790

BEN'S Shocking Invention

Franklin understood how electricity works. He wanted to figure out a way to protect houses from lightning. (Remember that then, most homes were made of wood. They caught fire easily if struck by lightning.)

The lightning rod is very simple. It is a metal rod attached to the top of a building. It is connected to the ground through a wire. The electric charge from the lightning strikes the rod. The charge follows the wire into the ground without harming the house or the people in it.

CAN GLOWING PLANTS
Light Up the Future?

Have you ever seen fireflies flitting through the evening air? Have you ever caught them in a jar? Have you used them as a nightlight? Fireflies are known as bioluminescent insects. They glow in the dark. Glowworms and anglerfish are two other bioluminescent animals.

A new kind of bioluminescent mushroom has been discovered in the forests of Brazil. Glowing fungi are also found in mountains and forests in North America and in temperate climates from Europe to Asia. Scientists are still working to understand them. Why do these fungi glow in the dark? Is it to attract insects? Is it to keep predators away? We do not yet know.

But, scientists have been able to transfer this glow-in-the-dark material to plants. Their goal is to develop trees that can also serve as streetlights!

WEIRD, WONDERFUL Plants

Earth is home to almost 400,000 species of plants. Some plants produce beautiful flowers. Some plants produce medicines that save lives. Others produce food. And, some plants . . . are just plain weird!

The baseball plant is native to South Africa. It has the same shape as a baseball. But, don't try to throw it. Unlike a baseball, the baseball plant is toxic and can cause serious skin problems.

The corpse flower is one of the world's largest flowers. It blooms about once every seven years. When it blooms, it can stand over 10 feet tall (3 m). You may not want to stand too close, though. The flower of the corpse plant smells like rotting animal flesh.

The giant water lily has round leaves that are often eight feet (2.4 m) across. The leaves are so large, a child can sit in one and float on the water. Its flowers have the sweet smell of pineapple.

But, not all plants are sweet like the giant water lily. Some plants bite back!

Read the titles. Scan
the texts. Look at the
pictures and chart. ①

What makes these
plants **WEIRD** and
WONDERFUL?

Plants That BITE BACK

④ Refer to the illustrations and photos to ask and answer questions about the texts.

What did you learn about plants that you did not know before?

VOCABULARY

bioluminescent:
a living organism that produces light

dew:
tiny drops of water that form on cool surfaces at night

species:
a group of plants or animals with similar characteristics

tentacle:
a hair on a plant that responds to touch

toxic:
poisonous

②

Read the texts. What questions do you have? Write them

- in the margins,
- in a notebook,
- or on self-stick notes.

Discuss the questions with others.

③

Meat-eating, or carnivorous, plants use sneaky tricks to catch their prey. These plants have developed traps to be able to eat and survive. The pitcher plant looks like a pitcher full of water. It has a sweet smell and a rich, red color that helps it attract its prey. Its favorite meal is insects. But, the pitcher plant has been known to eat frogs and mice too.

Sundew plants produce sweet droplets that look like dew shining in the sun. But, watch out, insects! It's a trap! The shiny dew is really glue. Some sundews have long tentacles. When an insect touches the tentacles, they snap the insect onto the sticky hairs of their center leaves. Once the insect is stuck, the plant begins to digest it.

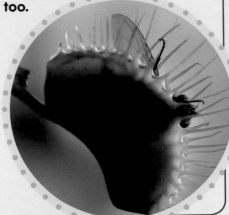

- Found: warm, wet regions around the world
- Grows: up to 10 inches tall
- Prey: dies in about 15 minutes
- Favorite food: mosquitoes
- Other use: old cough remedy

This meat-eating plant is a flypaper trap. Insects crawl onto its leaves and get stuck. Then, sticky tentacles fold around them and they are smothered. The bugs are fully digested in two to three weeks.

SUNDEW

VENUS
Flytrap

Perhaps the best known of all meat-eating plants is the Venus flytrap. The Venus flytrap has special jaw-like features called lobes. When an insect flies inside . . . snap! The lobes shut in less than half a second. So, if you walk by a Venus flytrap and see that its lobes are open, know that it's hungry and waiting for some prey. But, don't worry. The Venus flytrap has very select taste. It likes to feast on insects and spiders.

CAN GLOWING PLANTS
Light Up the Future?

Have you ever seen fireflies flitting through the evening air? Have you ever caught them in a jar? Have you used them as a nightlight? Fireflies are known as bioluminescent insects. They glow in the dark. Glowworms and anglerfish are two other bioluminescent animals.

A new kind of bioluminescent mushroom has been discovered in the forests of Brazil. Glowing fungi are also found in mountains and forests in North America and in temperate climates from Europe to Asia. Scientists are still working to understand them. Why do these fungi glow in the dark? Is it to attract insects? Is it to keep predators away? We do not yet know.

But, scientists have been able to transfer this glow-in-the-dark material to plants. Their goal is to develop trees that can also serve as streetlights!

WRITE ABOUT IT. ⑥
What uses can you think of for bioluminescent plants? How would you use bioluminescent plants to help the environment?

QUESTION to wonder
about information in the text

WEIRD, WONDERFUL Plants

Earth is home to almost 400,000 species of plants. Some plants produce beautiful flowers. Some plants produce medicines that save lives. Others produce food. And, some plants . . . are just plain weird!

The baseball plant is native to South Africa. It has the same shape as a baseball. But, don't try to throw it. Unlike a baseball, the baseball plant is toxic and can cause serious skin problems.

The corpse flower is one of the world's largest flowers. It blooms about once every seven years. When it blooms, it can stand over 10 feet tall (3 m). You may not want to stand too close, though. The flower of the corpse plant smells like rotting animal flesh.

The giant water lily has round leaves that are often eight feet (2.4 m) across. The leaves are so large, a child can sit in one and float on the water. Its flowers have the sweet smell of pineapple.

But, not all plants are sweet like the giant water lily. Some plants bite back!

Read the titles. Scan the texts. Look at the pictures and chart. ①
What makes these plants **WEIRD** and **WONDERFUL**?

Plants That **BITE BACK**

④ Refer to the illustrations and photos to ask and answer questions about the texts.

What did you learn about plants that you did not know before?

VOCABULARY

bioluminescent:
a living organism that produces light

dew:
tiny drops of water that form on cool surfaces at night

species:
a group of plants or animals with similar characteristics

tentacle:
a hair on a plant that responds to touch

toxic:
poisonous

②

Read the texts. What questions do you have? Write them
- in the margins,
- in a notebook,
- or on self-stick notes.

Discuss the questions with others.

③

Meat-eating, or carnivorous, plants use sneaky tricks to catch their prey. These plants have developed traps to be able to eat and survive. The pitcher plant looks like a pitcher full of water. It has a sweet smell and a rich, red color that helps it attract its prey. Its favorite meal is insects. But, the pitcher plant has been known to eat frogs and mice too.

Sundew plants produce sweet droplets that look like dew shining in the sun. But, watch out, insects! It's a trap! The shiny dew is really glue. Some sundews have long tentacles. When an insect touches the tentacles, they snap the insect onto the sticky hairs of their center leaves. Once the insect is stuck, the plant begins to digest it.

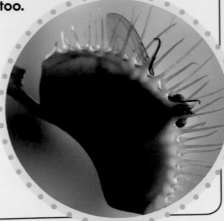

- Found: warm, wet regions around the world
- Grows: up to 10 inches tall
- Prey: dies in about 15 minutes
- Favorite food: mosquitoes
- Other use: old cough remedy

This meat-eating plant is a flypaper trap. Insects crawl onto its leaves and get stuck. Then, sticky tentacles fold around them and they are smothered. The bugs are fully digested in two to three weeks.

SUNDEW

VENUS
Flytrap

Perhaps the best known of all meat-eating plants is the Venus flytrap. The Venus flytrap has special jaw-like features called lobes. When an insect flies inside . . . snap! The lobes shut in less than half a second. So, if you walk by a Venus flytrap and see that its lobes are open, know that it's hungry and waiting for some prey. But, don't worry. The Venus flytrap has very select taste. It likes to feast on insects and spiders.

CAN GLOWING PLANTS
Light Up the Future?

Have you ever seen fireflies flitting through the evening air? Have you ever caught them in a jar? Have you used them as a nightlight? Fireflies are known as bioluminescent insects. They glow in the dark. Glowworms and anglerfish are two other bioluminescent animals.

A new kind of bioluminescent mushroom has been discovered in the forests of Brazil. Glowing fungi are also found in mountains and forests in North America and in temperate climates from Europe to Asia. Scientists are still working to understand them. Why do these fungi glow in the dark? Is it to attract insects? Is it to keep predators away? We do not yet know.

But, scientists have been able to transfer this glow-in-the-dark material to plants. Their goal is to develop trees that can also serve as streetlights!

WRITE ABOUT IT. ⑥
What uses can you think of for bioluminescent plants? How would you use bioluminescent plants to help the environment?

© Carson-Dellosa CD-104930

WEIRD, WONDERFUL Plants

Earth is home to almost 400,000 species of plants. Some plants produce beautiful flowers. Some plants produce medicines that save lives. Others produce food. And, some plants . . . are just plain weird!

The baseball plant is native to South Africa. It has the same shape as a baseball. But, don't try to throw it. Unlike a baseball, the baseball plant is toxic and can cause serious skin problems.

The corpse flower is one of the world's largest flowers. It blooms about once every seven years. When it blooms, it can stand over 10 feet tall (3 m). You may not want to stand too close, though. The flower of the corpse plant smells like rotting animal flesh.

The giant water lily has round leaves that are often eight feet (2.4 m) across. The leaves are so large, a child can sit in one and float on the water. Its flowers have the sweet smell of pineapple.

But, not all plants are sweet like the giant water lily. Some plants bite back!

Read the titles. Scan the texts. Look at the pictures and chart. ①

What makes these plants **WEIRD** and **WONDERFUL**?

Plants That **BITE BACK**

4 Refer to the illustrations and photos to ask and answer questions about the texts.

What did you learn about plants that you did not know before?

VOCABULARY

bioluminescent:
a living organism that produces light

dew:
tiny drops of water that form on cool surfaces at night

species:
a group of plants or animals with similar characteristics

tentacle:
a hair on a plant that responds to touch

toxic:
poisonous

2

Meat-eating, or carnivorous, plants use sneaky tricks to catch their prey. These plants have developed traps to be able to eat and survive. The pitcher plant looks like a pitcher full of water. It has a sweet smell and a rich, red color that helps it attract its prey. Its favorite meal is insects. But, the pitcher plant has been known to eat frogs and mice too.

Sundew plants produce sweet droplets that look like dew shining in the sun. But, watch out, insects! It's a trap! The shiny dew is really glue. Some sundews have long tentacles. When an insect touches the tentacles, they snap the insect onto the sticky hairs of their center leaves. Once the insect is stuck, the plant begins to digest it.

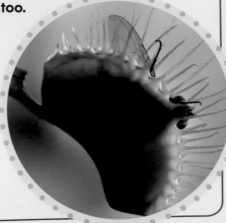

3 Read the texts. What questions do you have? Write them
- in the margins,
- in a notebook,
- or on self-stick notes.

Discuss the questions with others.

- Found: warm, wet regions around the world
- Grows: up to 10 inches tall
- Prey: dies in about 15 minutes
- Favorite food: mosquitoes
- Other use: old cough remedy

This meat-eating plant is a flypaper trap. Insects crawl onto its leaves and get stuck. Then, sticky tentacles fold around them and they are smothered. The bugs are fully digested in two to three weeks.

SUNDEW

VENUS
Flytrap

Perhaps the best known of all meat-eating plants is the Venus flytrap. The Venus flytrap has special jaw-like features called lobes. When an insect flies inside . . . snap! The lobes shut in less than half a second. So, if you walk by a Venus flytrap and see that its lobes are open, know that it's hungry and waiting for some prey. But, don't worry. The Venus flytrap has very select taste. It likes to feast on insects and spiders.

READ THE TEXTS AGAIN. ⑤
Put the facts together. What makes these plants unusual?

CAN GLOWING PLANTS
Light Up the Future?

Have you ever seen fireflies flitting through the evening air? Have you ever caught them in a jar? Have you used them as a nightlight? Fireflies are known as bioluminescent insects. They glow in the dark. Glowworms and anglerfish are two other bioluminescent animals.

A new kind of bioluminescent mushroom has been discovered in the forests of Brazil. Glowing fungi are also found in mountains and forests in North America and in temperate climates from Europe to Asia. Scientists are still working to understand them. Why do these fungi glow in the dark? Is it to attract insects? Is it to keep predators away? We do not yet know.

But, scientists have been able to transfer this glow-in-the-dark material to plants. Their goal is to develop trees that can also serve as streetlights!

WRITE ABOUT IT.
What uses can you think of for bioluminescent plants? How would you use bioluminescent plants to help the environment? ⑥

© Carson-Dellosa CD-104930

QUESTION to wonder
about information in the text

WEIRD, WONDERFUL Plants

Earth is home to almost 400,000 species of plants. Some plants produce beautiful flowers. Some plants produce medicines that save lives. Others produce food. And, some plants . . . are just plain weird!

The baseball plant is native to South Africa. It has the same shape as a baseball. But, don't try to throw it. Unlike a baseball, the baseball plant is toxic and can cause serious skin problems.

The corpse flower is one of the world's largest flowers. It blooms about once every seven years. When it blooms, it can stand over 10 feet tall (3 m). You may not want to stand too close, though. The flower of the corpse plant smells like rotting animal flesh.

The giant water lily has round leaves that are often eight feet (2.4 m) across. The leaves are so large, a child can sit in one and float on the water. Its flowers have the sweet smell of pineapple.

But, not all plants are sweet like the giant water lily. Some plants bite back!

Read the titles. Scan the texts. Look at the pictures and chart. ①

What makes these plants WEIRD and WONDERFUL?

Plants That **BITE BACK**

4 Refer to the illustrations and photos to ask and answer questions about the texts.

What did you learn about plants that you did not know before?

VOCABULARY

bioluminescent:
  a living organism that produces light

dew:
  tiny drops of water that form on cool surfaces at night

species:
  a group of plants or animals with similar characteristics

tentacle:
  a hair on a plant that responds to touch

toxic:
  poisonous

2

Meat-eating, or carnivorous, plants use sneaky tricks to catch their prey. These plants have developed traps to be able to eat and survive. The pitcher plant looks like a pitcher full of water. It has a sweet smell and a rich, red color that helps it attract its prey. Its favorite meal is insects. But, the pitcher plant has been known to eat frogs and mice too.

Sundew plants produce sweet droplets that look like dew shining in the sun. But, watch out, insects! It's a trap! The shiny dew is really glue. Some sundews have long tentacles. When an insect touches the tentacles, they snap the insect onto the sticky hairs of their center leaves. Once the insect is stuck, the plant begins to digest it.

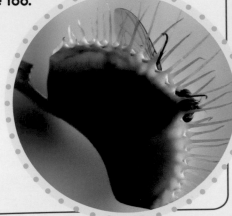

Read the texts. What questions do you have? Write them

- in the margins,
- in a notebook,
- or on self-stick notes.

Discuss the questions with others.

3

- Found: warm, wet regions around the world
- Grows: up to 10 inches tall
- Prey: dies in about 15 minutes
- Favorite food: mosquitoes
- Other use: old cough remedy

This meat-eating plant is a flypaper trap. Insects crawl onto its leaves and get stuck. Then, sticky tentacles fold around them and they are smothered. The bugs are fully digested in two to three weeks.

SUNDEW

VENUS
Flytrap

Perhaps the best known of all meat-eating plants is the Venus flytrap. The Venus flytrap has special jaw-like features called lobes. When an insect flies inside . . . snap! The lobes shut in less than half a second. So, if you walk by a Venus flytrap and see that its lobes are open, know that it's hungry and waiting for some prey. But, don't worry. The Venus flytrap has very select taste. It likes to feast on insects and spiders.

CAN GLOWING PLANTS
Light Up the Future?

Have you ever seen fireflies flitting through the evening air? Have you ever caught them in a jar? Have you used them as a nightlight? Fireflies are known as bioluminescent insects. They glow in the dark. Glowworms and anglerfish are two other bioluminescent animals.

A new kind of bioluminescent mushroom has been discovered in the forests of Brazil. Glowing fungi are also found in mountains and forests in North America and in temperate climates from Europe to Asia. Scientists are still working to understand them. Why do these fungi glow in the dark? Is it to attract insects? Is it to keep predators away? We do not yet know.

But, scientists have been able to transfer this glow-in-the-dark material to plants. Their goal is to develop trees that can also serve as streetlights!

WRITE ABOUT IT. ⑥
What uses can you think of for bioluminescent plants? How would you use bioluminescent plants to help the environment?

WEIRD, WONDERFUL Plants

Earth is home to almost 400,000 species of plants. Some plants produce beautiful flowers. Some plants produce medicines that save lives. Others produce food. And, some plants . . . are just plain weird!

The baseball plant is native to South Africa. It has the same shape as a baseball. But, don't try to throw it. Unlike a baseball, the baseball plant is toxic and can cause serious skin problems.

The corpse flower is one of the world's largest flowers. It blooms about once every seven years. When it blooms, it can stand over 10 feet tall (3 m). You may not want to stand too close, though. The flower of the corpse plant smells like rotting animal flesh.

The giant water lily has round leaves that are often eight feet (2.4 m) across. The leaves are so large, a child can sit in one and float on the water. Its flowers have the sweet smell of pineapple.

But, not all plants are sweet like the giant water lily. Some plants bite back!

Read the titles. Scan the texts. Look at the pictures and chart. ①
What makes these plants **WEIRD** and **WONDERFUL**?

Plants That **BITE BACK**

Read the texts. What questions do you have? Write them
- in the margins,
- in a notebook,
- or on self-stick notes.

Discuss the questions with others.

③

Meat-eating, or carnivorous, plants use sneaky tricks to catch their prey. These plants have developed traps to be able to eat and survive. The pitcher plant looks like a pitcher full of water. It has a sweet smell and a rich, red color that helps it attract its prey. Its favorite meal is insects. But, the pitcher plant has been known to eat frogs and mice too.

Sundew plants produce sweet droplets that look like dew shining in the sun. But, watch out, insects! It's a trap! The shiny dew is really glue. Some sundews have long tentacles. When an insect touches the tentacles, they snap the insect onto the sticky hairs of their center leaves. Once the insect is stuck, the plant begins to digest it.

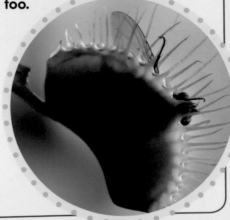

- Found: warm, wet regions around the world
- Grows: up to 10 inches tall
- Prey: dies in about 15 minutes
- Favorite food: mosquitoes
- Other use: old cough remedy

This meat-eating plant is a flypaper trap. Insects crawl onto its leaves and get stuck. Then, sticky tentacles fold around them and they are smothered. The bugs are fully digested in two to three weeks.

SUNDEW

Refer to the illustrations and photos to ask and answer questions about the texts.

④

What did you learn about plants that you did not know before?

VENUS
Flytrap

Perhaps the best known of all meat-eating plants is the Venus flytrap. The Venus flytrap has special jaw-like features called lobes. When an insect flies inside . . . snap! The lobes shut in less than half a second. So, if you walk by a Venus flytrap and see that its lobes are open, know that it's hungry and waiting for some prey. But, don't worry. The Venus flytrap has very select taste. It likes to feast on insects and spiders.

CAN GLOWING PLANTS

Light Up the Future?

Have you ever seen fireflies flitting through the evening air? Have you ever caught them in a jar? Have you used them as a nightlight? Fireflies are known as bioluminescent insects. They glow in the dark. Glowworms and anglerfish are two other bioluminescent animals.

A new kind of bioluminescent mushroom has been discovered in the forests of Brazil. Glowing fungi are also found in mountains and forests in North America and in temperate climates from Europe to Asia. Scientists are still working to understand them. Why do these fungi glow in the dark? Is it to attract insects? Is it to keep predators away? We do not yet know.

But, scientists have been able to transfer this glow-in-the-dark material to plants. Their goal is to develop trees that can also serve as streetlights!

WRITE ABOUT IT. ⑥
What uses can you think of for bioluminescent plants? How would you use bioluminescent plants to help the environment?

© Carson-Dellosa CD-104930

WEIRD, WONDERFUL Plants

Earth is home to almost 400,000 species of plants. Some plants produce beautiful flowers. Some plants produce medicines that save lives. Others produce food. And, some plants . . . are just plain weird!

The baseball plant is native to South Africa. It has the same shape as a baseball. But, don't try to throw it. Unlike a baseball, the baseball plant is toxic and can cause serious skin problems.

The corpse flower is one of the world's largest flowers. It blooms about once every seven years. When it blooms, it can stand over 10 feet tall (3 m). You may not want to stand too close, though. The flower of the corpse plant smells like rotting animal flesh.

The giant water lily has round leaves that are often eight feet (2.4 m) across. The leaves are so large, a child can sit in one and float on the water. Its flowers have the sweet smell of pineapple.

But, not all plants are sweet like the giant water lily. Some plants bite back!

Plants That **BITE BACK**

Meat-eating, or carnivorous, plants use sneaky tricks to catch their prey. These plants have developed traps to be able to eat and survive. The pitcher plant looks like a pitcher full of water. It has a sweet smell and a rich, red color that helps it attract its prey. Its favorite meal is insects. But, the pitcher plant has been known to eat frogs and mice too.

Sundew plants produce sweet droplets that look like dew shining in the sun. But, watch out, insects! It's a trap! The shiny dew is really glue. Some sundews have long tentacles. When an insect touches the tentacles, they snap the insect onto the sticky hairs of their center leaves. Once the insect is stuck, the plant begins to digest it.

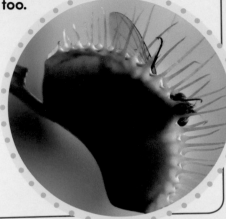

④ Refer to the illustrations and photos to ask and answer questions about the texts.

What did you learn about plants that you did not know before?

VOCABULARY

bioluminescent:
a living organism that produces light

dew:
tiny drops of water that form on cool surfaces at night

species:
a group of plants or animals with similar characteristics

tentacle:
a hair on a plant that responds to touch

toxic:
poisonous

②

③ Read the texts. What questions do you have? Write them
- in the margins,
- in a notebook,
- or on self-stick notes.

Discuss the questions with others.

- Found: warm, wet regions around the world
- Grows: up to 10 inches tall
- Prey: dies in about 15 minutes
- Favorite food: mosquitoes
- Other use: old cough remedy

This meat-eating plant is a flypaper trap. Insects crawl onto its leaves and get stuck. Then, sticky tentacles fold around them and they are smothered. The bugs are fully digested in two to three weeks.

SUNDEW

VENUS Flytrap

Perhaps the best known of all meat-eating plants is the Venus flytrap. The Venus flytrap has special jaw-like features called lobes. When an insect flies inside . . . snap! The lobes shut in less than half a second. So, if you walk by a Venus flytrap and see that its lobes are open, know that it's hungry and waiting for some prey. But, don't worry. The Venus flytrap has very select taste. It likes to feast on insects and spiders.

INTERESTING
Iditarod Info

- The fastest time is 8 days, 11 hours, 20 minutes, and 16 seconds. The slowest time is 32 days, 5 hours, 19 minutes, and 1 second.

- The ceremonial start is in Anchorage, Alaska. The official race begins in Willow, Alaska.

- There are two different courses. The race follows a northern route in even-numbered years. It follows a southern route in odd-numbered years.

- What happens when the weather is too warm and the trail starts to melt? The starting line can be moved to a "restart" location.

- There is a prize for last place. It is called the Red Lantern Award. It is a symbol of not giving up, no matter what, to achieve a goal.

WRITE ABOUT IT. **6**
What do you think is the most interesting thing about the Iditarod? Why?

© Carson-Dellosa CD-104930

QUESTION to wonder about information in the text

RACE ACROSS Alaska

The year was 1925. Imagine a dog pulling a sled over a snowy Alaskan trail. Time was critical. People in Nome had a bad disease. Who could get medicine there? Mushers and their faithful dogs could. This is the legacy of the Iditarod.

The Iditarod Trail Sled Dog Race was founded in 1973. It was started to keep Alaska dogsledding alive. It also recognized the Iditarod Trail as an historic trail.

On the first Saturday of March, mushers and their teams of dogs line up on the ceremonial starting line. They will take part in the "last great race on Earth." The race begins in Anchorage, Alaska. It covers about 1,000 miles (1,609 km) of rough mountain terrain. It ends in Nome, Alaska.

Each musher has a team of up to 16 dogs. Sometimes, dogs get tired or hurt and can no longer race. The team must finish with at least six dogs. Most teams end the race in fewer than 10 days.

1 Read the titles. Scan the texts. Look at the pictures and map.

Where do you think the **IDITAROD** takes place?

NORTHERN Dogs Only

Refer to the illustrations and photos to ask and answer questions about the texts.

④ Why do you think only certain kinds of dogs can be used in the Iditarod?

VOCABULARY

ceremonial:
done as part of a formal act

critical:
of highest importance

musher:
the driver of a dogsled

official:
formal

terrain:
the physical features of a stretch of land

②

Northern dogs such as huskies are best suited to race in the Iditarod. It is a rule that only northern dog breeds can race. Dogs need the right undercoat to be able to travel in such harsh conditions. Conditions would be too hard on most pet dogs.

The mushers are responsible for their teams of dogs. The dogs must wear a bootie on each of their feet. The booties protect the dogs' feet from being cut by hard-packed snow and ice.

Mushers and their dogs must check in at different points along the race. There are 26 checkpoints on the northern route. It doesn't matter which ones they stop at. But, they must stop at one for 24 hours. Two more eight-hour rest stops are required. The first thing mushers do when they stop at a checkpoint is feed and care for their dogs.

MUSH!

Each dog on the Iditarod team has a job. The lead dogs are the smartest and fastest. They run in the front. Swing dogs run behind lead dogs. Their job is to direct the team safely around turns. Wheel dogs are the biggest and strongest. They are placed right in front of the sled.

Mushers use spoken commands to lead the team. Here are some commands you would hear.

GEE means turn right.

HAW means turn left.

MUSH means go.

LINE OUT means the lead dog should pull straight ahead.

WHOA means stop.

Read the texts. What questions do you have? Write them
- in the margins,
- in a notebook,
- or on self-stick notes.

Discuss the questions with the group.

③

THE RACE TO NOME, ALASKA

Twice in its 43-year history (in 2003 and 2015), the race start moved to other locations due to unseasonably warm weather and a lack of snow.

NOME

Northern Route (Even Years)

Southern Route (Odd Years)

ANCHORAGE

INTERESTING
Iditarod Info

🐾 The fastest time is 8 days, 11 hours, 20 minutes, and 16 seconds. The slowest time is 32 days, 5 hours, 19 minutes, and 1 second.

🐾 The ceremonial start is in Anchorage, Alaska. The official race begins in Willow, Alaska.

🐾 There are two different courses. The race follows a northern route in even-numbered years. It follows a southern route in odd-numbered years.

🐾 What happens when the weather is too warm and the trail starts to melt? The starting line can be moved to a "restart" location.

🐾 There is a prize for last place. It is called the Red Lantern Award. It is a symbol of not giving up, no matter what, to achieve a goal.

WRITE ABOUT IT.
What do you think is the most interesting thing about the Iditarod? Why? ⑥

© Carson-Dellosa CD-104930

RACE ACROSS Alaska

The year was 1925. Imagine a dog pulling a sled over a snowy Alaskan trail. Time was critical. People in Nome had a bad disease. Who could get medicine there? Mushers and their faithful dogs could. This is the legacy of the Iditarod.

The Iditarod Trail Sled Dog Race was founded in 1973. It was started to keep Alaska dogsledding alive. It also recognized the Iditarod Trail as an historic trail.

On the first Saturday of March, mushers and their teams of dogs line up on the ceremonial starting line. They will take part in the "last great race on Earth." The race begins in Anchorage, Alaska. It covers about 1,000 miles (1,609 km) of rough mountain terrain. It ends in Nome, Alaska.

Each musher has a team of up to 16 dogs. Sometimes, dogs get tired or hurt and can no longer race. The team must finish with at least six dogs. Most teams end the race in fewer than 10 days.

Read the titles. Scan the texts. Look at the pictures and map. ①

Where do you think the **IDITAROD** takes place?

NORTHERN Dogs Only

④ Refer to the illustrations and photos to ask and answer questions about the texts.

Why do you think only certain kinds of dogs can be used in the Iditarod?

VOCABULARY

ceremonial:
  done as part of a formal act
critical:
  of highest importance
musher:
  the driver of a dogsled
official:
  formal
terrain:
  the physical features of a stretch of land

②

Northern dogs such as huskies are best suited to race in the Iditarod. It is a rule that only northern dog breeds can race. Dogs need the right undercoat to be able to travel in such harsh conditions. Conditions would be too hard on most pet dogs.

The mushers are responsible for their teams of dogs. The dogs must wear a bootie on each of their feet. The booties protect the dogs' feet from being cut by hard-packed snow and ice.

Mushers and their dogs must check in at different points along the race. There are 26 checkpoints on the northern route. It doesn't matter which ones they stop at. But, they must stop at one for 24 hours. Two more eight-hour rest stops are required. The first thing mushers do when they stop at a checkpoint is feed and care for their dogs.

MUSH!

Each dog on the Iditarod team has a job. The lead dogs are the smartest and fastest. They run in the front. Swing dogs run behind lead dogs. Their job is to direct the team safely around turns. Wheel dogs are the biggest and strongest. They are placed right in front of the sled.

Mushers use spoken commands to lead the team. Here are some commands you would hear.

GEE means turn right.

HAW means turn left.

MUSH means go.

LINE OUT means the lead dog should pull straight ahead.

WHOA means stop.

Read the texts. What questions do you have? Write them
- in the margins,
- in a notebook,
- or on self-stick notes.

Discuss the questions with the group.

③

THE RACE TO NOME, ALASKA

Twice in its 43-year history (in 2003 and 2015), the race start moved to other locations due to unseasonably warm weather and a lack of snow.

NOME

Northern Route (Even Years)

Southern Route (Odd Years)

ANCHORAGE

INTERESTING
Iditarod Info

🐾 The fastest time is 8 days, 11 hours, 20 minutes, and 16 seconds. The slowest time is 32 days, 5 hours, 19 minutes, and 1 second.

🐾 The ceremonial start is in Anchorage, Alaska. The official race begins in Willow, Alaska.

🐾 There are two different courses. The race follows a northern route in even-numbered years. It follows a southern route in odd-numbered years.

🐾 What happens when the weather is too warm and the trail starts to melt? The starting line can be moved to a "restart" location.

🐾 There is a prize for last place. It is called the Red Lantern Award. It is a symbol of not giving up, no matter what, to achieve a goal.

WRITE ABOUT IT.
What do you think is the most interesting thing about the Iditarod? Why? ⑥

© Carson-Dellosa CD-104930

RACE ACROSS Alaska

The year was 1925. Imagine a dog pulling a sled over a snowy Alaskan trail. Time was critical. People in Nome had a bad disease. Who could get medicine there? Mushers and their faithful dogs could. This is the legacy of the Iditarod.

The Iditarod Trail Sled Dog Race was founded in 1973. It was started to keep Alaska dogsledding alive. It also recognized the Iditarod Trail as an historic trail.

On the first Saturday of March, mushers and their teams of dogs line up on the ceremonial starting line. They will take part in the "last great race on Earth." The race begins in Anchorage, Alaska. It covers about 1,000 miles (1,609 km) of rough mountain terrain. It ends in Nome, Alaska.

Each musher has a team of up to 16 dogs. Sometimes, dogs get tired or hurt and can no longer race. The team must finish with at least six dogs. Most teams end the race in fewer than 10 days.

Read the titles. Scan the texts. Look at the pictures and map. ①

Where do you think the **IDITAROD** takes place?

NORTHERN Dogs Only

④ Refer to the illustrations and photos to ask and answer questions about the texts.

Why do you think only certain kinds of dogs can be used in the Iditarod?

VOCABULARY

ceremonial:
done as part of a formal act

critical:
of highest importance

musher:
the driver of a dogsled

official:
formal

terrain:
the physical features of a stretch of land

②

Northern dogs such as huskies are best suited to race in the Iditarod. It is a rule that only northern dog breeds can race. Dogs need the right undercoat to be able to travel in such harsh conditions. Conditions would be too hard on most pet dogs.

The mushers are responsible for their teams of dogs. The dogs must wear a bootie on each of their feet. The booties protect the dogs' feet from being cut by hard-packed snow and ice.

Mushers and their dogs must check in at different points along the race. There are 26 checkpoints on the northern route. It doesn't matter which ones they stop at. But, they must stop at one for 24 hours. Two more eight-hour rest stops are required. The first thing mushers do when they stop at a checkpoint is feed and care for their dogs.

MUSH!

Each dog on the Iditarod team has a job. The lead dogs are the smartest and fastest. They run in the front. Swing dogs run behind lead dogs. Their job is to direct the team safely around turns. Wheel dogs are the biggest and strongest. They are placed right in front of the sled.

Mushers use spoken commands to lead the team. Here are some commands you would hear.

GEE means turn right.

HAW means turn left.

MUSH means go.

LINE OUT means the lead dog should pull straight ahead.

WHOA means stop.

Read the texts. What questions do you have? Write them
- in the margins,
- in a notebook,
- or on self-stick notes.

Discuss the questions with the group.

③

THE RACE TO NOME, ALASKA

Twice in its 43-year history (in 2003 and 2015), the race start moved to other locations due to unseasonably warm weather and a lack of snow.

NOME

Northern Route (Even Years)

Southern Route (Odd Years)

ANCHORAGE

READ THE TEXTS AGAIN. ⑤

Put the facts together. Why is the Iditarod more than just a race?

INTERESTING
Iditarod Info

- 🐾 The fastest time is 8 days, 11 hours, 20 minutes, and 16 seconds. The slowest time is 32 days, 5 hours, 19 minutes, and 1 second.

- 🐾 The ceremonial start is in Anchorage, Alaska. The official race begins in Willow, Alaska.

- 🐾 There are two different courses. The race follows a northern route in even-numbered years. It follows a southern route in odd-numbered years.

- 🐾 What happens when the weather is too warm and the trail starts to melt? The starting line can be moved to a "restart" location.

- 🐾 There is a prize for last place. It is called the Red Lantern Award. It is a symbol of not giving up, no matter what, to achieve a goal.

WRITE ABOUT IT. ⑥
What do you think is the most interesting thing about the Iditarod? Why?

Carson-Dellosa CD-104930

QUESTION to wonder about information in the text

RACE ACROSS Alaska

The year was 1925. Imagine a dog pulling a sled over a snowy Alaskan trail. Time was critical. People in Nome had a bad disease. Who could get medicine there? Mushers and their faithful dogs could. This is the legacy of the Iditarod.

The Iditarod Trail Sled Dog Race was founded in 1973. It was started to keep Alaska dogsledding alive. It also recognized the Iditarod Trail as an historic trail.

On the first Saturday of March, mushers and their teams of dogs line up on the ceremonial starting line. They will take part in the "last great race on Earth." The race begins in Anchorage, Alaska. It covers about 1,000 miles (1,609 km) of rough mountain terrain. It ends in Nome, Alaska.

Each musher has a team of up to 16 dogs. Sometimes, dogs get tired or hurt and can no longer race. The team must finish with at least six dogs. Most teams end the race in fewer than 10 days.

Read the titles. Scan the texts. Look at the pictures and map. ①

Where do you think the **IDITAROD** takes place?

NORTHERN Dogs Only

VOCABULARY

ceremonial:
  done as part of a
  formal act
critical:
  of highest importance
musher:
  the driver of a dogsled
official:
  formal
terrain:
  the physical features
  of a stretch of land

2

Northern dogs such as huskies are best suited to race in the Iditarod. It is a rule that only northern dog breeds can race. Dogs need the right undercoat to be able to travel in such harsh conditions. Conditions would be too hard on most pet dogs.

The mushers are responsible for their teams of dogs. The dogs must wear a bootie on each of their feet. The booties protect the dogs' feet from being cut by hard-packed snow and ice.

Mushers and their dogs must check in at different points along the race. There are 26 checkpoints on the northern route. It doesn't matter which ones they stop at. But, they must stop at one for 24 hours. Two more eight-hour rest stops are required. The first thing mushers do when they stop at a checkpoint is feed and care for their dogs.

Read the texts. What questions do you have? Write them
  • in the margins,
  • in a notebook,
  • or on self-stick notes.

Discuss the questions with the group.

3

THE RACE TO NOME, ALASKA

Twice in its 43-year history (in 2003 and 2015), the race start moved to other locations due to unseasonably warm weather and a lack of snow.

Northern Route
(Even Years)

NOME

Southern Route
(Odd Years)

ANCHORAGE

READ THE TEXTS AGAIN. (5)
Put the facts together. Why is the Iditarod more than just a race?

INTERESTING
Iditarod Info

- 🐾 The fastest time is 8 days, 11 hours, 20 minutes, and 16 seconds. The slowest time is 32 days, 5 hours, 19 minutes, and 1 second.

- 🐾 The ceremonial start is in Anchorage, Alaska. The official race begins in Willow, Alaska.

- 🐾 There are two different courses. The race follows a northern route in even-numbered years. It follows a southern route in odd-numbered years.

- 🐾 What happens when the weather is too warm and the trail starts to melt? The starting line can be moved to a "restart" location.

- 🐾 There is a prize for last place. It is called the Red Lantern Award. It is a symbol of not giving up, no matter what, to achieve a goal.

WRITE ABOUT IT.
What do you think is the most interesting thing about the Iditarod? Why? (6)

QUESTION to wonder
about information in the text

RACE ACROSS Alaska

The year was 1925. Imagine a dog pulling a sled over a snowy Alaskan trail. Time was critical. People in Nome had a bad disease. Who could get medicine there? Mushers and their faithful dogs could. This is the legacy of the Iditarod.

The Iditarod Trail Sled Dog Race was founded in 1973. It was started to keep Alaska dogsledding alive. It also recognized the Iditarod Trail as an historic trail.

On the first Saturday of March, mushers and their teams of dogs line up on the ceremonial starting line. They will take part in the "last great race on Earth." The race begins in Anchorage, Alaska. It covers about 1,000 miles (1,609 km) of rough mountain terrain. It ends in Nome, Alaska.

Each musher has a team of up to 16 dogs. Sometimes, dogs get tired or hurt and can no longer race. The team must finish with at least six dogs. Most teams end the race in fewer than 10 days.

Read the titles. Scan the texts. Look at the pictures and map. (1)

Where do you think the **IDITAROD** takes place?

NORTHERN Dogs Only

④ Refer to the illustrations and photos to ask and answer questions about the texts.

Why do you think only certain kinds of dogs can be used in the Iditarod?

VOCABULARY

ceremonial:
   done as part of a formal act

critical:
   of highest importance

musher:
   the driver of a dogsled

official:
   formal

terrain:
   the physical features of a stretch of land

②

Northern dogs such as huskies are best suited to race in the Iditarod. It is a rule that only northern dog breeds can race. Dogs need the right undercoat to be able to travel in such harsh conditions. Conditions would be too hard on most pet dogs.

The mushers are responsible for their teams of dogs. The dogs must wear a bootie on each of their feet. The booties protect the dogs' feet from being cut by hard-packed snow and ice.

Mushers and their dogs must check in at different points along the race. There are 26 checkpoints on the northern route. It doesn't matter which ones they stop at. But, they must stop at one for 24 hours. Two more eight-hour rest stops are required. The first thing mushers do when they stop at a checkpoint is feed and care for their dogs.

Read the texts. What questions do you have? Write them
   • in the margins,
   • in a notebook,
   • or on self-stick notes.

Discuss the questions with the group.

③

THE RACE TO NOME, ALASKA

Twice in its 43-year history (in 2003 and 2015), the race start moved to other locations due to unseasonably warm weather and a lack of snow.

NOME

Northern Route (Even Years)

Southern Route (Odd Years)

ANCHORAGE

MUSH!

Each dog on the Iditarod team has a job. The lead dogs are the smartest and fastest. They run in the front. Swing dogs run behind lead dogs. Their job is to direct the team safely around turns. Wheel dogs are the biggest and strongest. They are placed right in front of the sled.

Mushers use spoken commands to lead the team. Here are some commands you would hear.

GEE means turn right.

HAW means turn left.

MUSH means go.

LINE OUT means the lead dog should pull straight ahead.

WHOA means stop.

INTERESTING
Iditarod Info

- The fastest time is 8 days, 11 hours, 20 minutes, and 16 seconds. The slowest time is 32 days, 5 hours, 19 minutes, and 1 second.

- The ceremonial start is in Anchorage, Alaska. The official race begins in Willow, Alaska.

- There are two different courses. The race follows a northern route in even-numbered years. It follows a southern route in odd-numbered years.

- What happens when the weather is too warm and the trail starts to melt? The starting line can be moved to a "restart" location.

- There is a prize for last place. It is called the Red Lantern Award. It is a symbol of not giving up, no matter what, to achieve a goal.

WRITE ABOUT IT.
What do you think is the most interesting thing about the Iditarod? Why? (6)

QUESTION to wonder about information in the text

RACE ACROSS Alaska

The year was 1925. Imagine a dog pulling a sled over a snowy Alaskan trail. Time was critical. People in Nome had a bad disease. Who could get medicine there? Mushers and their faithful dogs could. This is the legacy of the Iditarod.

The Iditarod Trail Sled Dog Race was founded in 1973. It was started to keep Alaska dogsledding alive. It also recognized the Iditarod Trail as an historic trail.

On the first Saturday of March, mushers and their teams of dogs line up on the ceremonial starting line. They will take part in the "last great race on Earth." The race begins in Anchorage, Alaska. It covers about 1,000 miles (1,609 km) of rough mountain terrain. It ends in Nome, Alaska.

Each musher has a team of up to 16 dogs. Sometimes, dogs get tired or hurt and can no longer race. The team must finish with at least six dogs. Most teams end the race in fewer than 10 days.

Read the titles. Scan the texts. Look at the pictures and map. (1)

Where do you think the **IDITAROD** takes place?

NORTHERN Dogs Only

VOCABULARY

ceremonial:
   done as part of a
   formal act
critical:
   of highest importance
musher:
   the driver of a dogsled
official:
   formal
terrain:
   the physical features
   of a stretch of land

②

Northern dogs such as huskies are best suited to race in the Iditarod. It is a rule that only northern dog breeds can race. Dogs need the right undercoat to be able to travel in such harsh conditions. Conditions would be too hard on most pet dogs.

The mushers are responsible for their teams of dogs. The dogs must wear a bootie on each of their feet. The booties protect the dogs' feet from being cut by hard-packed snow and ice.

Mushers and their dogs must check in at different points along the race. There are 26 checkpoints on the northern route. It doesn't matter which ones they stop at. But, they must stop at one for 24 hours. Two more eight-hour rest stops are required. The first thing mushers do when they stop at a checkpoint is feed and care for their dogs.

④ Refer to the illustrations and photos to ask and answer questions about the texts.

Why do you think only certain kinds of dogs can be used in the Iditarod?

MUSH!

Each dog on the Iditarod team has a job. The lead dogs are the smartest and fastest. They run in the front. Swing dogs run behind lead dogs. Their job is to direct the team safely around turns. Wheel dogs are the biggest and strongest. They are placed right in front of the sled.

Mushers use spoken commands to lead the team. Here are some commands you would hear.

GEE means turn right.

HAW means turn left.

MUSH means go.

LINE OUT means the lead dog should pull straight ahead.

WHOA means stop.

③ Read the texts. What questions do you have? Write them
   • in the margins,
   • in a notebook,
   • or on self-stick notes.
Discuss the questions with the group.

THE RACE TO NOME, ALASKA

Twice in its 43-year history (in 2003 and 2015), the race start moved to other locations due to unseasonably warm weather and a lack of snow.

Northern Route (Even Years)

NOME

Southern Route (Odd Years)

ANCHORAGE

READ THE TEXTS AGAIN. ⑤
Put the facts together. Why is the Iditarod more than just a race?

INTERESTING
Iditarod Info

🐾 The fastest time is 8 days, 11 hours, 20 minutes, and 16 seconds. The slowest time is 32 days, 5 hours, 19 minutes, and 1 second.

🐾 The ceremonial start is in Anchorage, Alaska. The official race begins in Willow, Alaska.

🐾 There are two different courses. The race follows a northern route in even-numbered years. It follows a southern route in odd-numbered years.

🐾 What happens when the weather is too warm and the trail starts to melt? The starting line can be moved to a "restart" location.

🐾 There is a prize for last place. It is called the Red Lantern Award. It is a symbol of not giving up, no matter what, to achieve a goal.

WRITE ABOUT IT.
What do you think is the most interesting thing about the Iditarod? Why? ⑥

QUESTION to wonder about information in the text

RACE ACROSS Alaska

The year was 1925. Imagine a dog pulling a sled over a snowy Alaskan trail. Time was critical. People in Nome had a bad disease. Who could get medicine there? Mushers and their faithful dogs could. This is the legacy of the Iditarod.

The Iditarod Trail Sled Dog Race was founded in 1973. It was started to keep Alaska dogsledding alive. It also recognized the Iditarod Trail as an historic trail.

On the first Saturday of March, mushers and their teams of dogs line up on the ceremonial starting line. They will take part in the "last great race on Earth." The race begins in Anchorage, Alaska. It covers about 1,000 miles (1,609 km) of rough mountain terrain. It ends in Nome, Alaska.

Each musher has a team of up to 16 dogs. Sometimes, dogs get tired or hurt and can no longer race. The team must finish with at least six dogs. Most teams end the race in fewer than 10 days.

Read the titles. Scan the texts. Look at the pictures and map. ①

Where do you think the **IDITAROD** takes place?

DISCUSSION Guide

1 What literary genre is this reader?

2 What things did the author do to get your attention?

3 Do you think this is an important topic? Explain with details from the texts.

4 How did you find the answers to the questions you had about the texts?

5 How did the author organize the information in this reader?

6 Why do you think the author chose this organization for the ideas she tells about in this **reader**?

7 What does the author want you to know about the US Postal Service?

8 How did the map help you better understand the role of the Pony Express?

9 Describe the Pony Express in three words or fewer.

10 What questions would you ask a Pony Express rider if he were alive today?

11 What was the author's purpose for writing this reader?

12 What other topic might you have added to this reader?

READE THE TEXTS AGAIN. ⑤

Put the facts together. Why is the Iditarod more than just a race?

INTERESTING
Iditarod Info

🐾 The fastest time is 8 days, 11 hours, 20 minutes, and 16 seconds. The slowest time is 32 days, 5 hours, 19 minutes, and 1 second.

🐾 The ceremonial start is in Anchorage, Alaska. The official race begins in Willow, Alaska.

🐾 There are two different courses. The race follows a northern route in even-numbered years. It follows a southern route in odd-numbered years.

🐾 What happens when the weather is too warm and the trail starts to melt? The starting line can be moved to a "restart" location.

🐾 There is a prize for last place. It is called the Red Lantern Award. It is a symbol of not giving up, no matter what, to achieve a goal.

WRITE ABOUT IT.
What do you think is the most interesting thing about the Iditarod? Why? ⑥

RACE ACROSS Alaska

The year was 1925. Imagine a dog pulling a sled over a snowy Alaskan trail. Time was critical. People in Nome had a bad disease. Who could get medicine there? Mushers and their faithful dogs could. This is the legacy of the Iditarod.

The Iditarod Trail Sled Dog Race was founded in 1973. It was started to keep Alaska dogsledding alive. It also recognized the Iditarod Trail as an historic trail.

On the first Saturday of March, mushers and their teams of dogs line up on the ceremonial starting line. They will take part in the "last great race on Earth." The race begins in Anchorage, Alaska. It covers about 1,000 miles (1,609 km) of rough mountain terrain. It ends in Nome, Alaska.

Each musher has a team of up to 16 dogs. Sometimes, dogs get tired or hurt and can no longer race. The team must finish with at least six dogs. Most teams end the race in fewer than 10 days.

Read the titles. Scan the texts. Look at the pictures and map. ①

Where do you think the **IDITAROD** takes place?

NORTHERN Dogs Only

VOCABULARY

ceremonial:
  done as part of a formal act
critical:
  of highest importance
musher:
  the driver of a dogsled
official:
  formal
terrain:
  the physical features of a stretch of land

②

Read the texts. What questions do you have? Write them
- in the margins,
- in a notebook,
- or on self-stick notes.

Discuss the questions with the group.

③

Northern dogs such as huskies are best suited to race in the Iditarod. It is a rule that only northern dog breeds can race. Dogs need the right undercoat to be able to travel in such harsh conditions. Conditions would be too hard on most pet dogs.

The mushers are responsible for their teams of dogs. The dogs must wear a bootie on each of their feet. The booties protect the dogs' feet from being cut by hard-packed snow and ice.

Mushers and their dogs must check in at different points along the race. There are 26 checkpoints on the northern route. It doesn't matter which ones they stop at. But, they must stop at one for 24 hours. Two more eight-hour rest stops are required. The first thing mushers do when they stop at a checkpoint is feed and care for their dogs.

THE RACE TO NOME, ALASKA

Twice in its 43-year history (in 2003 and 2015), the race start moved to other locations due to unseasonably warm weather and a lack of snow.

Northern Route (Even Years)

NOME

Southern Route (Odd Years)

ANCHORAGE

④ Refer to the illustrations and photos to ask and answer questions about the texts.

Why do you think only certain kinds of dogs can be used in the Iditarod?

MUSH!

Each dog on the Iditarod team has a job. The lead dogs are the smartest and fastest. They run in the front. Swing dogs run behind lead dogs. Their job is to direct the team safely around turns. Wheel dogs are the biggest and strongest. They are placed right in front of the sled.

Mushers use spoken commands to lead the team. Here are some commands you would hear.

GEE means turn right.

HAW means turn left.

MUSH means go.

LINE OUT means the lead dog should pull straight ahead.

WHOA means stop.

EARTH'S SOLE Satellite

1. How did the titles spark curiosity about the texts?

2. How do the texts relate to each other?

3. How did the questions in the titles help you understand the texts?

4. How do the photos and illustrations help you understand the texts?

5. What was your favorite part of this reader? Why?

6. How would you describe the topic to someone who has not read it?

7. What do you think the author thinks about the moon?

8. How did the author get your attention?

9. How did the way the author used words help you understand the texts?

10. What were three of the most important ideas in this informational reader?

11. What questions do you still have about the texts? How could you find answers to these questions?

12. How does this topic relate to your life?

DISCUSSION Guide

IT'S IN THE MAIL

PAR AVION

AIRMAIL

1. What literary genre is this reader?

2. What things did the author do to get your attention?

3. Do you think this is an important topic? Explain with details from the texts.

4. How did you find the answers to the questions you had about the texts?

5. How did the author organize the information in this reader?

6. Why do you think the author chose this organization for the ideas she tells about in this reader?

7. What does the author want you to know about the US Postal Service?

8. How did the map help you better understand the role of the Pony Express?

9. Describe the Pony Express in three words or fewer.

10. What questions would you ask a Pony Express rider if he were alive today?

11. What was the author's purpose for writing this reader?

12. What other topic might you have added to this reader?

1. What was the first thing you noticed about this reader?

2. What questions do you still have about Amelia Earhart? How would you find the answers to these questions?

3. How did the author get your attention?

4. How did you find the answers to the questions you had about the texts?

5. Why did the author think it was important for you to read about Amelia Earhart?

6. Why did the author include a text about Captain Katie Higgins?

7. How did the map help you understand the difficulty of Amelia's flight?

8. Describe Amelia Earhart's personality in three words.

9. What does the author want you to know about how air travel has changed?

10. What was the author's purpose in writing about this topic?

11. What do you think happened to Amelia Earhart?

12. How would you describe this reader to someone who has not read it?

1. What literary genre is this reader?

2. Why do you think the author chose this topic?

3. Describe Ben Franklin in three words.

4. What do you think the author's impression of Ben Franklin is?

5. How did the text features help you understand more about the subject?

6. What questions would you like to ask Benjamin Franklin if he were alive today?

7. Which of Franklin's inventions would you like to know more about? How could you find out?

8. How did the author get your attention?

9. What were three of the most important ideas in this informational reader?

10. What do you notice about the way the author used words?

11. How do the texts relate to each other?

12. Which of Franklin's contributions make your life better today?

WEIRD,
WONDERFUL
Plants

1. What makes these plants weird to you?

2. What makes these plants wonderful to you?

3. Why do you think the author chose this topic?

4. How did the author organize the information?

5. What did you learn about plants that you did not know before?

6. What organism would you like to see become bioluminescent?

7. How did the titles help you know what to expect from the texts?

8. How did the text features help you understand more about the topic?

9. What other questions do you have about the Venus flytrap?

10. What did the author do to interest you in the reader?

11. What was the author's purpose for writing this reader?

12. Which of these plants would you like to grow? Why?

DISCUSSION Guide

RACE ACROSS Alaska

1. What did you notice about how the author wrote the texts?

2. What was the first thing you noticed about this reader?

3. How did the author organize the information?

4. How did the map help you understand more about the Iditarod?

5. State the topic of these texts in three words or fewer.

6. How did the author make the texts interesting?

7. What would you want other readers to know about the texts in this reader?

8. What questions would you ask a musher if you had the chance?

9. If sled dogs could talk, what do you think they would say about running the Iditarod?

10. What was the author's purpose for writing this reader?

11. What else would you like to find out about the Iditarod?

12. Why do you think the legacy of the Iditarod lives on?

GUIDED READING MODEL

VOCABULARY

1

2

3

4

MY PREDICTIONS

MY OPINIONS

1

2

3

MY QUESTIONS

ASKING QUESTIONS

Ask questions before, during, and after reading
to understand the text better.

BEFORE READING

My questions

Answers I found

DURING READING

My questions

Answers I found

AFTER READING

My questions

Answers I found